English to Use

AGS PUBLISHING

by
Barbara A. Trautman
David H. Trautman

AGS Publishing
Circle Pines, Minnesota 55014-1796
1-800-328-2560

About the Authors

Barbara A. Trautman has taught English and social studies for more than thirty years at the elementary, secondary, and college levels. In addition, she has taught curriculum and methods courses for several universities. She holds a Ph.D. in curriculum and has served as curriculum coordinator in the United States and for American Overseas Schools sponsored by the State Department in Central America and Africa. She has also modeled the teaching of English as a second language in China.

David H. Trautman has been a professional writer of technical materials for industry and instructional materials for education. He holds a master's degree in education and has taught English, journalism, composition, and math to international students in Central America, Africa, and China.

Photo credits for this textbook can be found on page 304.

The publisher wishes to thank the following educators for their helpful comments during the review process for *English to Use*. Their assistance has been invaluable.

Patricia Baylis, Coordinator of Special Education, School District of Kansas City, Kansas City, MO; **Bonnie Gebhardt,** English Department Chairperson, El Cajon Valley High School, El Cajon, CA; **Pamela Kinzler,** Special Education Teacher, Penn Hills Senior High School, Pittsburgh, PA; **Virginia Malling,** Special Education Teacher, Oak Ridge High School, Oak Ridge, TN; **Suzanne Roth,** ELD Department Chairperson, La Quinta High School, Westminster, CA; **Susan West,** D/HH Instructor, Costa Mesa High School, Costa Mesa, CA

Publisher's Project Staff

Director, Product Development: Karen Dahlen; Associate Director, Product Development: Teri Mathews; Assistant Editor: Emily Kedrowski; Development Assistant: Bev Johnson; Senior Designer: Daren Hastings; Graphic Designer: Diane McCarty; Design Manager: Nancy Condon; Desktop Publishing Manager: Lisa Beller; Purchasing Agent: Mary Kaye Kuzma; Marketing Manager/Curriculum: Brian Holl

ASL Consultant: Daun-Teresa Wahl; ASL Illustrator: Judy King
Editorial and production services provided by The Mazer Corporation.

Printed in the United States of America
ISBN 0-7854-3056-3
Product Number 93600

A 0 9 8 7 6 5 4 3 2 1

Contents

How to Use This Book: A Study Guide

Welcome to *English to Use*. This book includes many of the grammar skills you will need now and later in life. You may be wondering why you should study English grammar. Think about the world around you. When you write, read, or speak, you draw on your knowledge of grammar. Knowing how to write sentences correctly will help you communicate more effectively, both in writing and speaking. Knowing how words fit together in sentences will help you understand what you read. We use language every day when we write, read, and speak. In this book, you will learn about the different parts of speech. You will learn about word placement and punctuation. You will put words together to create sentences and paragraphs.

As you read this book, notice how each lesson is organized. Information is presented and then followed by examples and activities. Read the information. Then practice what you have read. If you have trouble with a lesson, try reading it again.

It is important that you understand how to use this book before you start to read it. It is also important to know how to be successful in this course. The first section of the book can help you to achieve these things.

How to Study

These tips can help you study more effectively:

◆ Plan a regular time to study.

◆ Choose a quiet desk or table where you will not be distracted. Find a spot that has good lighting.

◆ Gather all the books, pencils, paper, and other equipment you will need to complete your assignments.

◆ Decide on a goal. For example: "I will finish reading and taking notes on Chapter 1, Lesson 1, by 8:00."

◆ Take a five- to ten-minute break every hour to keep alert.

◆ If you start to feel sleepy, take a break and get some fresh air.

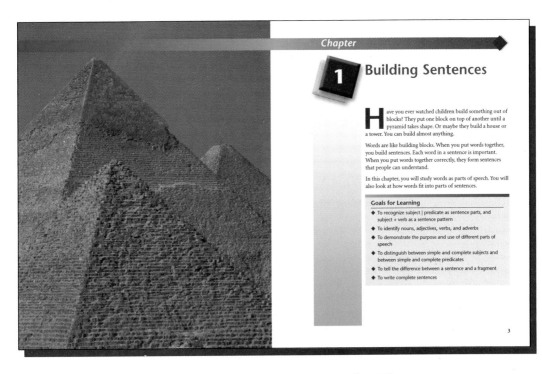

Chapter

1 Building Sentences

Have you ever watched children build something out of blocks? They put one block on top of another until a pyramid takes shape. Or maybe they build a house or a tower. You can build almost anything.

Words are like building blocks. When you put words together, you build sentences. Each word in a sentence is important. When you put words together correctly, they form sentences that people can understand.

In this chapter, you will study words as parts of speech. You will also look at how words fit into parts of sentences.

Goals for Learning
- To recognize subject | predicate as sentence parts, and subject + verb as a sentence pattern
- To identify nouns, adjectives, verbs, and adverbs
- To demonstrate the purpose and use of different parts of speech
- To distinguish between simple and complete subjects and between simple and complete predicates
- To tell the difference between a sentence and a fragment
- To write complete sentences

3

Before Beginning Each Chapter

◆ Read the chapter title and study the photograph. What does the photo tell you about the chapter title?

◆ Read the opening paragraphs.

◆ Study the Goals for Learning. The Chapter Review and tests will ask questions related to these goals.

◆ Look at the Chapter Review. The questions cover the most important information in the chapter.

Note these Features

Writing Tip
Quick tips to help improve writing skills

Writing Tip
Beware of double comparisons. Do not add *more* or *most* when you use the *-er* or *-est* form of an adjective.

Note
Hints or reminders that point out important information

Look for this box for helpful tips!

Using What You've Learned

Write five sentences comparing two or more movies, TV programs, or books. Compare the items with adjectives. When you have finished writing, check to make sure that you have used the correct comparative or superlative form of each adjective.

Using What You've Learned
An exercise that practices something taught in the chapter

Communication Connection

Body language is communicating by moving your body parts. It includes crossing your arms, tapping your feet, and eye contact.

Communication Connection
Information about various ways people communicate with each other

Before Beginning Each Lesson

Read the lesson title and restate it in the form of a question.

For example, write:
What is writing mechanics?

Look over the entire lesson, noting the following:

◆ bold words

◆ text organization

◆ exercises

◆ notes in the margins

◆ photos

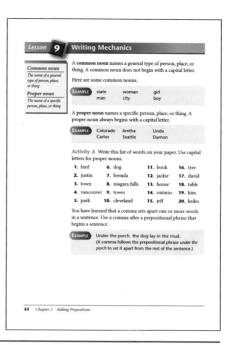

As You Read the Lesson

◆ Read the major headings.

◆ Read the paragraphs that follow.

◆ Read the content in the Example boxes.

◆ Before moving on to the next lesson, see if you understand the concepts you read. If you do not, reread the lesson. If you are still unsure, ask for help.

◆ Practice what you have learned by doing the activities in each lesson.

Using the Bold Words

Bold type

Words seen for the first time will appear in bold type

Glossary

Words listed in this column are also found in the glossary

Knowing the meaning of all the boxed words in the left column will help you understand what you read.

These words appear in **bold type** the first time they appear in the text and are often defined in the paragraph.

A **common noun** names a general type of person, place, thing, or idea.

All of the words in the left column are also defined in the **glossary**.

Common noun—(kom´ ən noun) The name of a general type of person, place, thing, or idea. (p. 44)

Word Study Tips

◆ Start a vocabulary file with index cards to use for review.

◆ Write one word on the front of each card. Write the chapter number, lesson number, and definition on the back.

◆ You can use these cards as flash cards by yourself or with a study partner to test your knowledge.

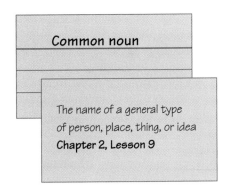

Common noun

The name of a general type of person, place, thing, or idea
Chapter 2, Lesson 9

Using the Reviews

◆ In the Chapter Reviews, answer the questions about vocabulary under Part A. Study the words and definitions. Say them aloud to help you remember them.

◆ Answer the questions under the other parts of the Chapter Reviews.

◆ Review the Test-Taking Tips.

Preparing for Tests

◆ Complete the activities in each lesson. Make up similar activity questions to practice what you have learned. You may want to do this with a classmate and share your questions.

◆ Review your answers to lesson activities and Chapter Reviews.

◆ Test yourself on vocabulary words and key ideas.

◆ Use graphic organizers as study tools.

Writing Practice

◆ Read and review Appendix A: The Writing Process at the back of this book.

◆ Follow the directions outlined in each step of the process. For example, read the information under Prewriting. Choose a topic you feel strongly about. Gather information to develop a paper about that topic.

◆ Write a first draft on your topic. Then revise and proofread your draft.

◆ Share your draft with others and ask for their opinions. Using your comments and your readers' comments, rewrite your draft.

◆ Read and revise your second draft. Proofread it and revise it again as needed.

◆ When your paper is final, share it with others. Also, take the time to evaluate what you have written. Ask yourself, "What would I do differently next time?"

American Sign Language (ASL) Illustrations

Many people with hearing impairments rely on hand signs and gestures to communicate. They use a language called American Sign Language (ASL). In each chapter, you will learn some ASL signs for words or sentences that appear in the lessons. Look at the word order in the ASL sentences. It is different than sentences in the English language. ASL has grammar rules that are different from the English language. Read and review Appendix B: ASL Illustrations.

Using Graphic Organizers

A graphic organizer is a visual representation of information. It can help you see how ideas are related to each other. A graphic organizer can help you study for a test or organize information before you write. Here are some examples.

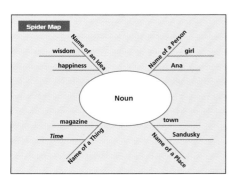

Spider Map

The Spider Map shown here can be used to connect related ideas to a central idea or concept. Write the main or central idea or concept in the circle in the center. Identify related ideas and write them on the lines that angle out from the circle. Write examples that support the ideas on the horizontal lines that are attached to the angled lines.

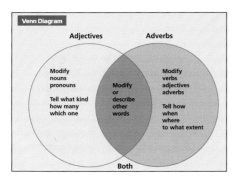

Venn Diagram

The Venn diagram shown here can be used to compare and contrast two things. For example, this diagram compares and contrasts adjectives and adverbs. List the characteristics for adjectives in the left circle. List the characteristics for adverbs in the right circle. In the intersection of the two circles, list the characteristics that both have.

Introduction

Whenever you speak or write, you use language to communicate. The English language is made up of letters and sounds arranged in patterns to form words. Words are arranged in patterns to form sentences. Groups of sentences form paragraphs. Groups of paragraphs form stories, articles, reports, letters, and so on. Using the English language correctly will help you to communicate correctly.

Each word in the English language is a part of speech. In this book, you will learn about:

Nouns	Words that name people, places, and things
Pronouns	Words that take the place of nouns
Verbs	Words that show action or state-of-being
Adjectives	Words that describe nouns or pronouns
Adverbs	Words tell about verbs, adjectives, or other adverbs
Prepositions	Words that relate nouns and pronouns to other words in a sentence
Conjunctions	Words that connect words and ideas
Interjections	Words that show strong feelings

As you learn about the parts of speech, you will learn how they work in sentences. You will also learn how to arrange the parts of speech to form different sentence patterns. Sentence variety adds interest to any type of writing you do.

Communication is important. Hearing people use spoken words to communicate in the English language. Many people with hearing impairments rely on hand signs and gestures to communicate. They use a language called American Sign Language (ASL). Each chapter of this book will help you to communicate better in English. In each chapter, you will also learn some ASL signs for words or sentences that appear in the lessons. Appendix B shows the ASL alphabet and many of the words or sentences you will learn in sign language. Clear communication can connect people with one another both in words and in signs.

Building Sentences

Have you ever watched children build something out of blocks? They put one block on top of another until a pyramid takes shape. Or maybe they build a house or a tower. You can build almost anything.

Words are like building blocks. When you put words together, you build sentences. Each word in a sentence is important. When you put words together correctly, they form sentences that people can understand.

In this chapter, you will study words as parts of speech. You will also look at how words fit into parts of sentences.

Goals for Learning

◆ To recognize subject | predicate as sentence parts, and subject + verb as a sentence pattern

◆ To identify nouns, adjectives, verbs, and adverbs

◆ To demonstrate the purpose and use of different parts of speech

◆ To distinguish between simple and complete subjects and between simple and complete predicates

◆ To tell the difference between a sentence and a fragment

◆ To write complete sentences

Sentence
A group of words that forms a complete thought; a sentence begins with a capital letter and ends with a period, question mark, or exclamation point

Subject
The part of a sentence that tells who or what the sentence is about

Predicate
The part of a sentence that tells what the subject is doing

Capital letter
A letter that is uppercase. A is a capital or uppercase letter; a is a lowercase letter

Period (.)
The punctuation mark ending a sentence that makes a statement or gives a command

Question mark (?)
A punctuation mark that ends a sentence asking a question

Exclamation point (!)
A punctuation mark showing strong feeling

People speak and write in sentences. A **sentence** is a group of words that tells a complete idea. A sentence has a **subject** and a **predicate.** The subject is the part of a sentence that tells who or what the sentence is about. The predicate is the part of a sentence that tells what the subject is doing.

Every sentence begins with a **capital letter,** or uppercase letter. Every sentence ends with a **period (.),** a **question mark (?),** or an **exclamation point (!).**

> **EXAMPLE** **Sentence**   Teams win.
> **Sentence parts**   subject | predicate
> (*Teams* is the subject of the sentence. *Teams* tells what the sentence is about. *Win* is the predicate in the sentence. *Win* tells what the subject is doing.)

Activity A Write these sentences on your paper. Label the subject and predicate in each sentence.

1. Birds sing.

2. Cats climb.

3. Tools break.

4. Cars run.

5. Teams play.

Activity B Write a different one-word predicate for each of these subjects. Write the complete sentences on your paper.

1. Boys _____ .

2. People _____ .

3. Women _____ .

4. Waves _____ .

5. Wolves _____ .

Sentence pattern

The basic form of a sentence

Activity C Write a different one-word subject for each of these predicates. Write the complete sentences on your paper.

1. _____ grow.

2. _____ sit.

3. _____ roar.

4. _____ walk.

5. _____ sing.

To find the subject of a sentence, first look for the verb. Then ask who or what is doing the action.

The order of words in a sentence is important. The English language has patterns of word order in sentences. In this lesson, you have been reading and writing the first **sentence pattern,** subject and verb. A sentence pattern is the basic form of a sentence.

EXAMPLE   Sentence   Teams win.

              Sentence pattern   subject + verb

Activity D Copy the sentences. Fill in the blanks on your paper.

1. A sentence has two parts. The two parts are the _____ and the _____ .

2. Read this sentence:
Students write.

Students is the _____ of the sentence, and *write* is the _____ of the sentence.

3. The sentence pattern is _____ + _____ .

These students write their test answers.

Noun

A word that names a person, place, or thing

Every word in the English language is a part of speech. A **noun** is a part of speech. Nouns are words that name. A noun names a person, a place, or a thing. The subject of a sentence is usually a noun.

> EXAMPLE
>
> | **Sentence** | Citizens vote. |
> |---|---|
> | **Sentence parts** | subject \| predicate |
> | **Sentence pattern** | subject + verb |
>
> (*Citizens* is a noun that tells the name of persons.)
>
> | **Sentence** | Towns grow. |
> |---|---|
> | **Sentence parts** | subject \| predicate |
> | **Sentence pattern** | subject + verb |
>
> (*Towns* is a noun that tells the name of places.)
>
> | **Sentence** | Telephones ring. |
> |---|---|
> | **Sentence parts** | subject \| predicate |
> | **Sentence pattern** | subject + verb |
>
> (*Telephones* is a noun that tells the name of things.)

Activity A Find the nouns in these sentences. Write the nouns on your paper.

1. Leaders plan.

2. Clowns laugh.

3. Artists paint.

4. Children play.

5. Swimmers float.

Activity B Find the noun in each group. Write the nouns on your paper.

1. write author sing

2. build govern nation

3. man eat find

4. table sit think

5. buy tape remember

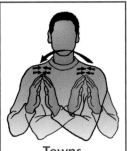

Towns

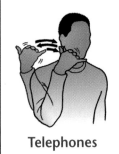

Telephones

Activity C Write each sentence on your paper. Underline the nouns.

1. Fires burn.
2. Trumpets blare.
3. Mice squeak.
4. Trees grow.
5. Winds blow.
6. Lightning strikes.
7. Snow falls.
8. Glass breaks.
9. Flowers droop.
10. Needles hurt.

Activity D Find the nouns in these sentences. Write each noun on your paper and tell whether it names a *person, place,* or *thing.*

1. Chains rattle.
2. Pilots fly.
3. Stereos play.
4. Cities grow.
5. Leaders speak.

Activity E Answer each of these items on your paper.

1. Nouns tell the names of persons, _____ , or _____ .
2. Write the nouns in this list:

house	car	did	flowers
day	driver	streets	teacher
books	person	cloud	town
horse	chairs	tell	sit

3. Write five nouns of your own that name places.
4. Write five nouns of your own that tell the names of persons.
5. Write five nouns of your own that name things.

Lesson 3 | Adjectives

Adjective

A word that describes a noun

An **adjective** is a part of speech. Adjectives describe nouns. An adjective gives information about a noun.

EXAMPLE

Good teams win.

Parts of speech	adjective noun verb
Sentence parts	subject	predicate
Sentence pattern	subject + verb

(*Teams* is a noun. *Good* is an adjective used to describe the noun *teams*. *Good* tells what kind of teams.)

Activity A Write each sentence on your paper. Circle the adjectives. Draw a line under each noun. All these sentences use the subject + verb pattern.

1. Little birds sing.   **4.** Big ships sail.

2. Hungry wolves howl.   **5.** Empty cars sit.

3. White clouds float.

Nouns can have many adjectives that describe them.

EXAMPLE   Friendly, happy, noisy children played.

Activity B Write each sentence on your paper. Circle the adjectives. Draw a line under each noun.

1. Long, yellow pencils break.

2. Ripe, red apples fall.

3. Strong, young women win.

4. Loud cars race.

5. Weary men sleep.

Article

*A word that points out
a noun*

A, an, and *the* are **articles.** Articles are adjectives. Articles point out nouns. Use *an* before words beginning with *a, e, i, o, u,* and sometimes *h.* Use *a* before words beginning with the other letters. Use *the* before any letter.

EXAMPLE   An ant crawls.   A frog jumps.   The wind blows.

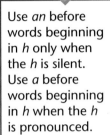

Use *an* before words beginning in *h* only when the *h* is silent. Use *a* before words beginning in *h* when the *h* is pronounced.

Activity C Write the article that belongs with each sentence on your paper.

1. (A, An) deer runs.

2. (An, A) old man sleeps.

3. (An, The) best team wins.

4. (The, A) egg hatches.

5. (The, An) summer breeze blows.

Activity D Add an adjective to each sentence. You may choose from the list below or think of your own. Write the complete sentences on your paper.

a	good	loud	the
an	great	old	tired
big	healthy	pretty	wild
brave	little	strong	young

1. _____ sirens squeal.

2. _____ people walk.

3. _____ bug crawls.

4. _____ flowers bloom.

5. _____ horses run.

6. _____ artist draws.

7. _____ soldiers fight.

8. _____ farmers plant.

9. _____ athletes run.

10. _____ singers perform.

Lesson 4 Action Verbs

Verb

A word that shows action

Action verb

A word that tells what the subject of a sentence does

A **verb** is a word that shows action. Verbs tell what is happening in a sentence. The predicate of a sentence always has a verb.

Action verbs tell what the subject does.

EXAMPLE

Good teams win.

Parts of speech	adjective noun verb
Sentence parts	subject	predicate
Sentence pattern	subject + verb

(*Win* tells what the teams do. *Win* is an action verb.)

Activity A Write each sentence on your paper. Draw a line under each action verb.

1. The red rooster crows.
2. The golden sun rises.
3. An old, rusty bell clangs.
4. A lonely bird sings.
5. A new day dawns.

Action verbs do not always show action or movement.

EXAMPLE

The tired child sleeps.
(*Sleeps* is an action verb. It does not show action or movement, but it still tells what the child—the subject—does.)

Activity B Write each sentence on your paper. Draw a line under each action verb.

1. The gray kitten breathes.
2. The drowsy owls stare.
3. A wise old man sits.
4. An athlete rests.
5. Little children dream.

Activity C Complete each sentence with an action verb that makes sense. Choose one of the verbs in the box below or think of your own. Write the complete sentences on your paper.

cries	strikes	sets	laughs
rises	hops	reads	jokes
grows	races	studies	plays

1. The white rabbit _____ .

2. The red sun _____ .

3. A lost child _____ .

4. The student _____ .

5. Bright lightning _____ .

Activity D Write each sentence on your paper. Label each word a noun (*n.*), an adjective (*adj.*), or a verb (*v.*).

Example   An eel slithers.
                 adj. n.   v.

1. The young racehorse trots.

2. A fat robin chirps.

3. An owl sleeps.

4. A friend waves.

5. A black kitten drinks.

Activity E Write the answer to each question.

1. What does a noun tell?

2. What does an adjective tell?

3. What three words are articles?

4. What does a verb tell?

5. What does an action verb tell?

Adverb

A word that describes a verb, an adjective, or another adverb

An **adverb** is a word that describes a verb, an adjective, or another adverb. When an adverb describes a verb, it tells how, when, or where. In this lesson, adverbs tell *how* about verbs.

> **EXAMPLE**
>
> Good teams practice eagerly.
>
> | | | | | |
> | **Parts of speech** | *adj.* | *noun* | *verb* | *adverb* |
> | **Sentence parts** | subject | predicate | | |
> | **Sentence pattern** | subject + verb | | | |
>
> (The adverb *eagerly* tells **how** good teams practice. *Eagerly* is an adverb that describes the verb *practice*. *Eagerly* is part of the predicate.)

Activity A Write each sentence on your paper. Circle each adverb. Draw a line under the verb it tells about.

1. The brown deer ran swiftly.

2. The train whistle blows loudly.

3. The snow falls quickly.

4. The bus moves rapidly.

5. The couple dances gracefully.

All of the adverbs in Activity A come after the verb. Adverbs do not always come after a verb. An adverb that describes the verb is always part of the predicate, no matter where the adverb is in the sentence.

> **EXAMPLE**
>
> The red fox | ran swiftly.
>
> | | | | | |
> | **Parts of speech** | *adj.* | *adj.* *noun* | *verb* | *adverb* |
> | **Sentence parts** | | subject | predicate | |
>
> subject
>
> Swiftly, | the red fox | ran.
>
> predicate
>
> (The adverb *swiftly* tells **how** about the verb *ran* in both sentences. *Swiftly* is separated from the verb *ran* in the second sentence, but it is still part of the predicate.)

Activity B Write the Activity A sentences again. This time, begin each sentence with the adverb.

All of the adverbs in Activity A end in *-ly.* Some examples of adverbs that do not end in *-ly* are *fast, hard,* and *well.* These adverbs usually come after the verb.

Activity C Write each sentence on your paper. Draw a line under the verb. Circle the adverb.

1. The whole team plays hard.

2. The track star runs fast.

3. The man dresses well.

4. The teacher spoke fast.

5. The young people work hard.

People sometimes mix up the words *good* and *well. Good* is usually an adjective. *Well* is usually an adverb.

> ### Writing Tip
>
> Besides *good* and *well,* people often confuse *bad* and *badly* and *real* and *really. Bad* and *real* are adjectives. *Badly* and *really* are adverbs.

Activity D In these sentences, *well* is an adverb and *good* is an adjective. Write these sentences on your paper. Label each word a noun (*n.*), a verb (*v.*), an adjective (*adj.*), or an adverb (*adv.*).

Example The new car runs well.
            adj. adj. n. v. adv.

1. A good idea does well.

2. Good steak cooks well.

3. A good old recipe works well.

4. A good student learns well.

5. A good car drives well.

Adverbs tell how, when, or where an action happens. In this lesson, adverbs tell *when* about verbs.

> **EXAMPLE**
>
> The good teams practice daily.
>
> **Parts of speech**   adj.   adj.   noun   verb   adverb
> **Sentence parts**   subject | predicate
> **Sentence pattern**   subject + verb
> (*Daily* is an adverb that describes the verb *practice*. *Daily* tells **when** the good teams practice.)

Activity A Write each sentence on your paper. Circle each adverb. Draw a line under each verb.

1. The jet plane lands today.
2. The wide river floods often.
3. The guest arrives tomorrow.
4. The old bus stops twice.
5. The TV show runs late.
6. A good worker tries again.
7. The mail comes early.
8. The morning paper comes late.
9. A good friend arrives today.
10. The clock stops sometimes.
11. The store closes soon.
12. The sick child coughs often.
13. A little girl laughs first.
14. A kind nurse visits daily.
15. The angry dog barks now.

As you learned in Lesson 5, adverbs do not always come after the verb. Some sentences begin with adverbs.

EXAMPLE   Today, the helicopter lands.
           (*Today* is an adverb telling when the
           helicopter lands.)

Activity B Write the Activity A sentences again. Begin each sentence with the adverb. Write the new sentences on your paper.

Sometimes adverbs come right before the verb.

EXAMPLE   The detectives often travel.
           (*Often* is an adverb telling when the
           detectives travel.)

A sentence can have more than one adverb. Adverbs can begin or end a sentence. An adverb can come before or after the verb.

EXAMPLE   The train always arrives late. Travelers wait
           sometimes. Often travelers leave.

Activity C Write each sentence on your paper. Circle each adverb. Draw a line under each verb. Some sentences may have more than one adverb.

1. The baseball game starts late.
2. The pitcher suddenly throws.
3. The batter swings once.
4. A player runs fast.
5. Soon the best team wins.
6. The band sometimes practices daily.
7. Often, the drummer arrives first.
8. Twice, the guitar player came early.
9. The band always practices late.
10. Tomorrow, the band has a show.

Adverbs tell how, when, or where an action happens. In this lesson, adverbs tell *where* about verbs.

EXAMPLE

The good teams play there.

	adj.	adj.	noun	verb	adverb
Parts of speech	adj.	adj.	noun	verb	adverb
Sentence parts	subject	predicate			
Sentence pattern	subject + verb				

(*There* tells where the good teams play. *There* is an adverb that describes the verb *play*.)

Activity A Write each sentence on your paper. Circle the adverb. Draw a line under the verb.

1. Life goes on.

2. A football player falls down.

3. The fire truck drives nearby.

4. The computer sits downstairs.

5. An airplane flies above.

6. A young couple goes out.

7. A sick man rests upstairs.

8. We discuss new topics here.

9. A big dog barks outside.

10. The days speed by.

11. The cat stays inside.

12. The tall woman points there.

13. A small plane flew around.

14. The group follows along.

15. The sleepy captain goes below.

Activity B Read each sentence and find each adverb. Write each adverb on your paper. Write whether the adverb tells *how, when,* or *where*. Some sentences may have more than one adverb.

1. Suddenly, news arrives.

2. People often talk.

3. News travels fast.

4. Ships rarely sink.

5. Often, planes arrive early.

6. Space shuttles speed skyward.

7. Good news reads well.

8. Trains run slowly.

9. Speed records move up quickly.

10. Sometimes, the computer screen goes blank.

Activity C Number your paper from 1 to 10. Read each sentence and find all the adverbs. Write the adverbs on your paper. Some sentences may have more than one adverb.

1. Tonight, the late TV show starts early.

2. The old movie stars act well.

3. The pilot flies alone.

4. His instruments work poorly.

5. His fuel runs low.

6. Suddenly, a rescue ship comes.

7. The pilot leaves safely.

8. Finally, he smiles happily.

9. Then the TV show ends quickly.

10. The silly ad runs twice.

You have learned that every sentence has a subject and a predicate. The **complete subject** is the whole part of the sentence that tells who or what the sentence is about. The **simple subject** is the one or more main nouns or pronouns in the sentence.

Complete subject

The whole part of a sentence that tells who or what the sentence is about

Simple subject

One or more subject nouns or pronouns in a sentence

Complete predicate

The whole part of a sentence that tells what the subject is doing

Simple predicate

One or more verbs in a sentence

The **complete predicate** is the whole part of the sentence that tells what the subject is doing. The **simple predicate** is the one or more main verbs in the predicate.

EXAMPLE   Good, strong teams play hard.
Sentence parts   subject | predicate
(*Teams* is the simple subject. *Good, strong teams* is the complete subject. *Play* is the simple predicate. *Play hard* is the complete predicate.)

Sometimes the simple subject is also the complete subject. Sometimes the simple predicate is also the complete predicate.

EXAMPLE   Teams play.
Sentence parts   subject | predicate
(*Teams* is the simple subject and also the complete subject. *Play* is the simple predicate and also the complete predicate.)

Activity A Write each sentence on your paper. Draw a line under the complete subject. Circle the complete predicate.

1. The rusty car clatters loudly.
2. A skilled worker finishes quickly.
3. The old bicycle breaks suddenly.
4. The tired men work hard.
5. The summer sun shines brightly.

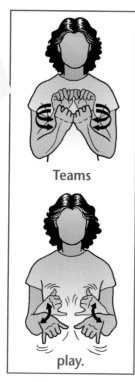

Teams

play.

Teams play.

Activity B The complete subject is underlined in each of the following sentences. Number your paper from 1 to 5. Write the simple subject in each complete subject.

1. The black smoke drifts up.
2. A red car stops suddenly.
3. The new clothes fit nicely.
4. A hungry cat eats quickly.
5. A graceful white swan swims fast.

Activity C The complete predicate is underlined in each of the following sentences. Number your paper from 1 to 5. Write the simple predicate in each complete predicate.

1. The kind teacher grades easily.
2. The sharp pencil writes well.
3. The old jeans fade nicely.
4. The large theater quickly fills.
5. The orange leaves fall slowly.

Activity D Copy these sentences on your paper. Underline the complete subject once and the complete predicate twice. Circle the simple subject and simple predicate.

1. The large mall fills quickly.
2. A bright, young couple shops carefully.
3. The small child cries loudly.
4. Shiny, new products sell easily.
5. A polite guard helps quietly.

Fragment

*A group of words that is
not a complete sentence*

Not every group of words tells a complete idea. A group
of words that does not tell a complete idea is a **fragment.**
A fragment is missing a subject or a predicate. Because a
fragment does not tell a complete idea, it is not a sentence.

EXAMPLE **Fragment**   Good, strong teams.
(What happened to *Good, strong teams?*
This fragment is missing a predicate.)

Fragment   Play hard.
(Who or what *Play hard?* This fragment is missing
a subject.)

Sentence   Good, strong teams play hard.

Activity A On your paper, write the groups of words that are
complete sentences. Begin each sentence with a capital letter.
End each sentence with a period.

1. kites fly
2. the young people
3. small, distant kites
4. other people watch
5. long kite string
6. flying high
7. the boys play
8. clear, sunny day
9. the wind blows
10. children run

11. it goes far
12. fun there
13. new cars
14. cars race
15. the finish line
16. friends cheer
17. the day ends
18. adults relax
19. a dark night
20. everybody sleeps

Do not let a fragment stand by itself. Include it in a sentence with the word or words it describes or explains.

Activity B Decide whether each group of words is missing a subject or a predicate. Complete each fragment and write it as a sentence on your paper.

1. a tall, thin boy
2. drove yesterday
3. dropped quickly
4. the happy woman
5. big, white waves

Activity C Read the short passage. Then follow the directions.

> A big, red kite. An old green kite rises slowly. Suddenly, the long string breaks. Disappears quickly.

1. Find two fragments in the passage. Copy them on your paper. Next to each fragment, write whether it is missing a subject or a predicate.

2. Complete each fragment to make it a sentence. Add a subject or predicate. Write the new sentences on your paper.

3. Find two complete sentences in the passage. Copy them on your paper.

4. Underline the complete subject once and the complete predicate twice in each of the complete sentences. Circle each simple subject and simple predicate.

5. On your paper, rewrite the passage using your new sentences.

Punctuation

Marks in a sentence that tell readers when to pause or stop

Comma (,)

A punctuation mark used to set apart one or more words

You have learned that each sentence begins with a capital letter and ends with a period, a question mark, or an exclamation point. These marks are types of **punctuation.** Punctuation marks are marks that tell readers when to pause or stop.

Commas are another kind of punctuation. We use them in a sentence to set apart one or more words. A comma tells you to pause briefly.

A comma can separate two or more adjectives in a sentence.

> **EXAMPLE** The new, red truck crashed.
> (The comma separates *new* and *red. New* and *red* are two adjectives that tell about the noun *truck.*)

Activity A Write each sentence on your paper. Add commas to separate adjectives.

1. A beautiful sunny day dawned.

2. The young lean athlete ran.

3. The excited friendly crowd cheered.

4. A new happy coach watched.

5. The bright shiny medal sparkled.

You can use a comma after an adverb at the beginning of a sentence.

> **EXAMPLE** Cheerfully, the bird sang.
> (The comma separates the adverb *cheerfully* from the rest of the sentence.)

Write a description of an activity you enjoy, such as a sport or game. Choose lively action verbs to tell what happens. Include adverbs to explain how, when, or where. Use interesting adjectives to describe nouns. Circle the verbs. Underline the adverbs once and the adjectives twice.

Activity B Write each sentence on your paper. Add commas after adverbs at the beginning of sentences.

1. Sadly the lost boy cries.

2. Immediately a police officer arrives.

3. Soon a crowd gathers around.

4. Nervously the parents search.

5. Happily the family hugs.

Activity C Write each sentence on your paper. Add commas where necessary.

1. The long winding road curves sharply.

2. Usually people drive slowly.

3. A new young driver crashes.

4. Luckily the driver walks away.

5. Softly the driver apologizes.

Activity D Write the following sentences on your paper. Begin each sentence with a capital letter. End each sentence with a period. Add commas where necessary.

1. dark heavy clouds gather

2. loud noisy thunder crashes

3. soon lightning strikes

4. the scared worried people rush inside

5. suddenly rain falls

Lightning strikes Earth fifty to one hundred times every second of the day.

Chapter 1   R E V I E W

Word Bank

action verb

article

comma

exclamation point

period

predicate

question mark

sentence pattern

subject

verb

Part A Use the words from the Word Bank to complete sentences 1–10.

1. A punctuation mark showing strong feeling is an _____ .
2. A _____ is the basic form of a sentence.
3. The part of a sentence that tells what the subject is doing is the _____ .
4. An _____ is a word that points out a noun.
5. A punctuation mark ending a sentence that makes a statement or gives a command is a _____ .
6. A _____ is a word that shows action.
7. A word that tells what the subject of a sentence does is an _____ .
8. The part of a sentence that tells who or what the sentence is about is the _____ .
9. A _____ is a punctuation mark that ends a sentence asking a question.
10. A _____ is a punctuation mark used to set apart one or more words.

Part B Write each sentence on your paper. Underline the complete subject. Circle the complete predicate.

11. The bright, blue truck slows down.
12. A young doctor studies quietly.
13. The new car stops suddenly.
14. The sleepy dog lies down.

Part C List the nouns, adjectives, and adverbs in these sentences on your paper. Some sentences may have more than one adjective. For each adverb, write whether it tells *how, when,* or *where.*

15. The radio station plays softly.
16. Rock music videos entertain everywhere.
17. The old, worn-out stereo speakers crackle loudly.
18. New electric guitars play well.

Part D Decide whether each group of words is a sentence or a fragment. Write *sentence* or *fragment* on your paper.

19. New music videos.

20. A new lamp.

21. Rusty hinges creak.

22. Computer software helps.

Part E Write each sentence correctly on your paper. The sentences need capital letters and end punctuation. Some sentences need commas.

23. the skillful builder works hard

24. the tired worker tries again

25. suddenly the new saw breaks

26. carefully the worker saws again

Part F On your paper, write the letter that correctly identifies the simple subject or simple predicate in each sentence.

27. The young boy shouts loudly. (simple subject)

    A The young boy   **C** young boy

    B boy   **D** shouts

28. The cold, hard wind blows. (simple subject)

    A The cold, hard wind   **C** cold, hard wind

    B blows   **D** wind

29. The wild wolves suddenly howl. (simple predicate)

    A The wild wolves   **C** howl

    B wolves   **D** suddenly howl

30. Slowly, snow falls. (simple predicate)

    A Slowly   **C** snow

    B Slowly falls   **D** falls

Test-Taking Tip When answering multiple-choice questions, first identify the answers you know are incorrect.

2

Adding Prepositions

Have you ever thought about the words you use to give directions or to explain a process? You might tell someone that the kitchen is *down* the hall or *beside* the dining room. Perhaps you have explained how to make a sandwich. You might have used words such as *of, on, under,* and *in.* These words show the relationships between the items on the sandwich. You might have said, "First, get two slices *of* bread. Put a slice *of* cheese *on* the bread. Then, place some lettuce *under* the tomato. Now hold the sandwich *in* your hands."

In Chapter 2, you will learn about prepositions—words that show the relationships between things. You will also discover how prepositional phrases make sentences more interesting by telling *which one, what kind, how, when,* and *where.*

Goals for Learning

◆ To identify and use prepositions and prepositional phrases

◆ To state the use of prepositional phrases

◆ To tell the difference between prepositions and adverbs

◆ To identify state-of-being verbs

◆ To use capital letters with proper nouns

◆ To use a comma to set off an introductory prepositional phrase

Preposition

A word that ties or relates a noun or pronoun to another part of the sentence

Prepositional phrase

A group of words that begins with a preposition and ends with a noun or pronoun

Object of the preposition

The noun or pronoun that follows the preposition in a prepositional phrase

A **preposition** is a word that ties or relates a noun or pronoun to another part of the sentence.

A **prepositional phrase** is a group of words that begins with a preposition and ends with a noun or pronoun. The noun or pronoun that follows the preposition is the **object of the preposition.**

EXAMPLE | Natasha looked at the truck.

Parts of speech   noun   verb   prep.   adj.   noun

(The preposition *at* begins the prepositional phrase *at the truck.* The noun *truck* is the object of the preposition *at.*)

Different prepositions show a different relationship between words in a sentence. Notice how the meaning of the sentence changes when the preposition changes.

EXAMPLE | Natasha looked inside the truck.
Natasha looked under the truck.
Natasha looked behind the truck.

Here are some common prepositions.

aboard	behind	from	since
about	below	in	through
above	beneath	inside	to
across	beside	into	toward
after	between	near	under
against	beyond	of	until
along	by	off	up
among	down	on	upon
around	during	outside	with
at	except	over	within
before	for	past	without

With

In

Between

Across

Activity A Add a different preposition to each of the following sentences. Write each sentence on your paper.

1. Arturo walked _____ the woods.
2. They talked _____ the music video.
3. We sat _____ the shady tree.
4. The plane flew _____ the clouds.
5. The principal spoke _____ the new students.
6. Lisa jumped _____ the big puddle.
7. The dog ran _____ the yard.
8. A boy waited _____ the park bench.
9. Pete looked _____ the little house.
10. They watched _____ their friends.

As you have seen, prepositions help you add more information to your sentences. Prepositional phrases make your sentences complete and more interesting.

> **EXAMPLE**   The girls swam.
> The girls swam in the pool.
> (The prepositional phrase *in the pool* adds information to the sentence *The girls swam.*)

Activity B Add a prepositional phrase from the box to each sentence. Write the new sentences on your paper. Use each phrase only once.

| near the car | along the shore | with her best friend |
| for two hours | around the block | |

1. We searched.
2. Rain fell.
3. They talked.
4. Matt drove.
5. Kim walked.

Adjective prepositional phrase

A prepositional phrase that describes a noun

A prepositional phrase can be an adjective phrase or an adverb phrase.

An **adjective prepositional phrase** acts like an adjective in a sentence. Like an adjective, an adjective prepositional phrase describes a noun. It answers the questions *which one* or *what kind* about a noun.

EXAMPLE   The red pencil with an eraser broke.

Parts of speech   adj. adj. noun prep. adj. noun verb

(The preposition *with* shows the relationship of *eraser* to *red pencil*. *With an eraser* is an adjective prepositional phrase that answers the question *which red pencil broke?* The red pencil with an eraser broke.)

The woman in the car laughed.

Parts of speech   adj. noun prep. adj. noun verb

(The preposition *in* shows the relationship of *car* to *woman*. *In the car* is an adjective prepositional phrase that answers the question *which woman laughed?* The woman in the car laughed.)

Remember that the complete subject is the whole part of the sentence that tells who or what the sentence is about. The simple subject is the one or more subject nouns or pronouns in a sentence.

An adjective prepositional phrase that tells about the simple subject is part of the complete subject.

EXAMPLE

Sentence parts   complete subject   predicate

The woman in the car laughed.

simple subj.   adj. prep. phrase

(The adjective prepositional phrase *in the car* describes the simple subject *woman*, a noun.)

Activity A Each of these sentences has an adjective prepositional phrase that describes the simple subject. Write each sentence on your paper. Underline the adjective phrase. Circle the noun it describes.

Example A small (boy) <u>with glasses</u> spoke softly.

1. A dog inside the house barked.

2. A scared woman with a child hurried outside.

3. The firefighters from town arrived quickly.

4. A big player with the ball ran swiftly.

5. People in the stands cheered loudly.

A prepositional phrase includes the preposition, the object of the preposition, and all of the words in between. Adjectives that come between a preposition and its object tell about the object.

> **EXAMPLE** A green parrot in the tall palm tree blinked.
> **Prepositional phrase** in the tall palm tree
> **Parts of speech** *prep. adj. adj. adj. noun*
> (The adjectives *the, tall,* and *palm* all tell about the noun *tree,* the object of the preposition *in*. The adjectives *A* and *green* tell about the noun *parrot,* the simple subject of the sentence.)

Activity B Write each sentence on your paper. Underline the adjective prepositional phrase. Circle the noun it describes. Draw an arrow from each adjective to the noun it describes.

Example Small (shadows) <u>under the large tree</u> danced.

1. The strong men in the canoe paddled quickly.

2. Smoke from the big, bright fires drifted upward.

3. The huge pile of wood disappeared.

4. Small boys with happy faces ran swiftly.

5. Three small children on the blanket watched quietly.

Prepositional phrases often come between the simple subject and the verb in a sentence. Don't let the noun or pronoun that is the object of the preposition confuse you. The object of a preposition is *never* the subject of a sentence.

To find the simple subject of a sentence, follow these steps.

1. Find the verb.

2. Ask who or what is doing the action.

3. Find the noun or pronoun that answers the who or what question about the verb.

4. Do not include nouns or pronouns that are part of a prepositional phrase.

> A prepositional phrase can sometimes act as a noun and act as the subject of a sentence.
>
> *Example* Behind the chair is a good hiding place.

EXAMPLE

Sentence parts   *complete subject*   *complete predicate*

The man with the hat sings well.

simple subject   *verb*

(The words *man* and *hat* are nouns in the complete subject. To find out which noun is the simple subject, ask the question *who sings well?* The man with the hat sings well. *Man* is the simple subject. *Hat* is the object of the preposition *with*. The adjective prepositional phrase *with the hat* describes the noun *man*.)

Activity A Write each sentence on your paper. Circle the prepositional phrase. Underline the simple subject.

1. The plant with yellow leaves died.

2. The yellow leaves of the dead plant fell gently.

3. The plant near the window grew well.

4. Light from the big window shines brightly.

5. Flowers on the plant opened wide.

Some nouns name groups of people or things.

EXAMPLE

group	audience	flock	herd
crowd	bunch	collection	class

When an adjective prepositional phrase follows a word that names a group, you may become confused about which noun is the subject. Remember, the object of a preposition is *never* the subject of a sentence.

EXAMPLE

Sentence parts

complete subject   complete predicate

A small school of fish swam past.

simple subject obj. of prep. verb

(*What swam past?* Although *fish* answers the question, *fish* cannot be the subject because it is the object of the preposition *of*. The noun *school* is the simple subject. The adjective prepositional phrase *of fish* describes the noun *school*.)

A *quartet* is a group of four.

Activity B Write each sentence on your paper. Circle the prepositional phrase. Underline the simple subject.

1. The quartet of men sang loudly.

2. The silent herd of cows moved slowly.

3. A large group of students gathered.

4. The collection of fine jewels sparkled.

5. Packs of wild dogs howled.

Activity C Write each sentence on your paper. Fill in the blank with a prepositional phrase to fit the sentence. Underline the simple subject.

1. A team _____ arrived.

2. The happy crowd _____ yelled wildly.

3. A swarm _____ buzzed.

4. A big flock _____ flew away.

5. The fans _____ cheered loudly.

Adverb prepositional phrase

A prepositional phrase that describes a verb

An **adverb prepositional phrase** acts like an adverb in a sentence. Like an adverb, an adverb prepositional phrase answers the questions *how, when,* and *where* about a verb.

> **EXAMPLE**
>
> Many athletes run quickly on the track.
>
> **Parts of speech**   *adj.* *noun* *verb* *adv.* *prep.* *adj.* *noun*
>
> (The preposition *on* shows the relationship of *track* to *run*. *On the track* is an adverb prepositional phrase that answers the question *where do many athletes run quickly?* Many athletes run quickly on the track.)
>
> The four students left during the play.
>
> **Parts of speech**   *adj.* *adj.* *noun* *verb* *prep.* *adj.* *noun*
>
> (The preposition *during* shows the relationship of *play* to *left*. *During the play* is an adverb prepositional phrase that answers the question *when did the students leave?* The students left during the play.)

You have learned that the complete predicate is the whole part of the sentence that tells what the subject is doing. The simple predicate, or verb, is the main verb in the predicate.

An adverb prepositional phrase that tells about the verb is part of the complete predicate.

> **EXAMPLE**
>
> **Sentence parts**   *subject*   *complete predicate*
>
> Many athletes run at top speed.
>
>   *verb* *prep. phrase*
>
> (The adverb prepositional phrase *at top speed* describes the simple predicate *run*. It answers the question *how did the athletes run?* The athletes ran at top speed.)

The sun rises

above

the mountains.

The sun rises above
the mountains.

Activity A Each of these sentences has an adverb prepositional phrase. Write each sentence on your paper. Underline the adverb phrase. Circle the verb it describes. Next to each sentence, write whether the adverb phrase answers *when* or *where* about the verb.

Example The cowhands (camped) near the mountain.
Where?

1. The campfire burns brightly during the meal.
2. The tired cowhands talk after dinner.
3. Night creeps over the land.
4. Stars shine across the sky.
5. A hot meal bubbles in the pot.
6. Wolves howl through the still night.
7. Embers glow until morning.
8. The sun rises above the mountains.
9. The birds sing in the trees.
10. Another day begins on the range.

Activity B Write each sentence on your paper. Fill in the blank with an adverb prepositional phrase that answers the question in parentheses about the verb. Then underline each verb.

1. Rick drove directly _____ . (Where?)
2. My mom works _____ . (When?)
3. The talented musician played _____ . (How?)
4. That woman shops daily _____ . (Where?)
5. The newborn kitten crawled _____ . (Where?)

Some words that are prepositions can also be adverbs. Remember, a preposition always has an object. An adverb does not have an object.

> **EXAMPLE**
>
> **Adverb** The football players ran around.
>
> **Adverb** The football players ran
> **prepositional phrase** around the field.
>
> (In the first sentence, *around* does not have an object. It is an adverb that describes how the football players ran. In the second sentence, *around* has an object—*field. Around* is a preposition that introduces the adverb prepositional phrase *around the field.*)

Activity A Write each word in bold on your paper. Write whether it is an *adverb* or a *preposition.*

1. The cat looked **around.**
2. The bus traveled **around** the block.
3. The car parked **outside** the gate.
4. The girls waited **outside.**
5. The ball rolled **down** the stairs.

Activity B Write the sentences on your paper. Draw one line under the adverb. Draw two lines under the prepositional phrase. Circle the verb.

Example The woman (goes) out for dinner.

1. The driver of the car slows down in seconds.
2. The car stops across from our house.
3. The car sits up on a jack.
4. A bus rattles by past the car.
5. A tow truck comes along after a few minutes.

Activity C On your paper, complete each sentence with a word from the box. First use the word as an adverb. Then use the word as a preposition that introduces an adverb prepositional phrase. Do not use a word more than once.

after	before	down	near	outside
around	behind	inside	out	up

Example   We drove _____ .
                We drove around.
                We drove around the town.

1. The curious boy looked _____ .

2. The happy children walked _____ .

3. A small, green frog jumped _____ .

4. The painter climbed _____ .

5. The clumsy clown fell _____ .

Communication Connection

Instant messaging is a way to communicate directly and quickly with others on the computer. People use it at home to chat with friends or family members. At work, people use it to share and discuss the latest news and information with people in distant places.

Activity D Write each sentence on your paper. Circle the prepositional phrase. Above each phrase, write whether it is an adjective phrase or an adverb phrase. Draw an arrow to the subject or the verb that each phrase tells about.

Example
                Adv. phrase
    A baby yelled loudly (at midnight.)

           Adj. phrase
    A box (of popcorn) spilled outside.

1. The kind doctor from the village sent his friend an instant message.

2. The good friend responded immediately with a greeting.

3. The strong swimmer dove beneath the waves.

4. Ten boxes of books arrived.

5. A small, green bird whistled loudly for its mate.

Sentences often have more than one prepositional phrase. Sometimes the phrases describe the same word.

A sentence may have more than one adjective phrase.

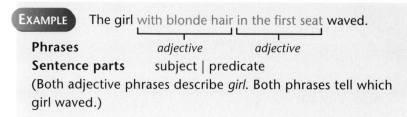

EXAMPLE   The girl with blonde hair in the first seat waved.

Phrases   adjective   adjective
Sentence parts   subject | predicate
(Both adjective phrases describe *girl*. Both phrases tell which girl waved.)

A sentence may have more than one adverb phrase.

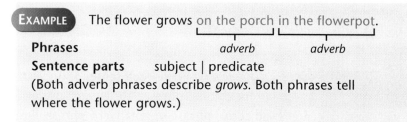

EXAMPLE   The flower grows on the porch in the flowerpot.

Phrases   adverb   adverb
Sentence parts   subject | predicate
(Both adverb phrases describe *grows*. Both phrases tell where the flower grows.)

A sentence may have adjective phrases and adverb phrases.

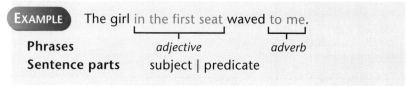

EXAMPLE   The girl in the first seat waved to me.

Phrases   adjective   adverb
Sentence parts   subject | predicate

You have learned about adjective prepositional phrases that describe subjects. An adjective prepositional phrase may also describe the noun object of another prepositional phrase.

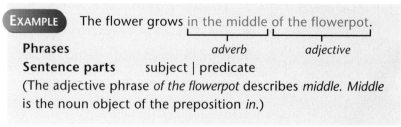

EXAMPLE   The flower grows in the middle of the flowerpot.

Phrases   adverb   adjective
Sentence parts   subject | predicate
(The adjective phrase *of the flowerpot* describes *middle*. *Middle* is the noun object of the preposition *in*.)

Activity A On your paper, write each prepositional phrase. Then write the word each phrase describes.

1. Ducks swam through the pond toward the grass.
2. Flowers sit beneath the window in the garden.
3. People waited against the fence after the game and talked among themselves.
4. A lazy cat sleeps beside the pillow on the big bed.
5. The old TV broke in the middle of a good show.
6. The car with the number on the side stopped.
7. The man walked down the street into the park.
8. The people stood in the hall outside the door.
9. The dog ran between the tree and the bush on the hill.
10. The new computer sits among the other packages in the lab.

Activity B On your paper, write the prepositional phrases in each sentence. Next to each phrase write *adjective phrase* or *adverb phrase* and the word the phrase describes.

Example   Shoppers with heavy coats hurry to the stores in the city.

with heavy coats—adjective phrase, shoppers
to the stores—adverb phrase, hurry
in the city—adjective phrase, stores

1. A clerk with a smile on his face works quietly at the computer.
2. Another clerk sorts through a stack of paper carefully.
3. A huge amount of work for other people piles on the desks.
4. A long line of people waits nervously for reports on the new project.
5. The computer clerks in the office work hard through the long hours of the day.

State-of-being verb

A verb that tells that the subject exists, but does not show action

You have learned that an action verb is a word that shows action. There is another kind of verb. It is a **state-of-being verb.** A state-of-being verb tells that the subject exists in some way. A state-of-being verb does not show action.

The most commonly used state-of-being verb is *to be.* Here are some forms of the verb *to be.*

am	is	were
are	was	will be

Here are some other state-of-being verbs.

appear	feel	remain
become	look	seem

Because a state-of-being verb does not show action, you may have difficulty finding the verb when it is followed by an adverb prepositional phrase. Remember:

- A verb is never part of a prepositional phrase.
- A prepositional phrase always begins with a preposition.

EXAMPLE   The team is on the field.

Sentence parts   *subject verb adverb phrase*
Sentence pattern   subject + verb
(*Is* is a verb. The verb *is* does not show action. It tells that the team exists. It is a *state-of-being verb.* The preposition *on* begins the prepositional phrase *on the field.*)

Activity A Write each sentence on your paper. Underline the state-of-being verb. Circle the prepositional phrase.

1. Jack is behind the tree.   **4.** They appear friendly.

2. I am in big trouble.   **5.** His book is under his desk.

3. The car remained clean.

Look in a newspaper or a magazine article for five sentences with state-of-being verbs. Could an action verb make any of these sentences more interesting? Write the five sentences that you chose on your paper. Replace the state-of-being verbs with action verbs and rewrite the sentences.

Activity B Write each sentence on your paper. Circle the prepositional phrases. Draw one line under the subject noun. Draw two lines under the state-of-being verb.

Example A <u>can</u> (of beans) <u>was</u> (on the shelf.)

1. A loaf of bread is in the oven.
2. My friends were in the other room.
3. The smell of the warm bread is in the air.
4. My parents were in the basement.
5. Soon, only bread crumbs will be on the plate.

Good writers often use action verbs instead of state-of-being verbs. Action verbs make sentences clearer and more interesting than state-of-being verbs do.

> **EXAMPLE**
>
> **State-of-being verb**   The runner is on the track.
> **Action verb**   The runner races on the track.
> (The action verb *races* gives readers a clearer picture of what the runner is doing on the track.)

Activity C Write these sentences on your paper. Circle the state-of-being verb in each sentence. Then write the sentence again, using an action verb in place of the state-of-being verb. Try to use a different action verb in each sentence.

1. The pitcher is on the mound.
2. The catcher is behind the plate.
3. Yesterday, Jane was in center field.
4. I am in the stands.
5. Other players are in their dugouts.

Prepositional phrases may come anywhere in a sentence. An adjective phrase usually follows the noun it describes. An adverb phrase may come before or after the verb it tells about.

EXAMPLE

Sentence parts

adv. phrase   *subject*   *adj.phrase*

On the street, a bus with a flat tire stops near our school.

verb   *adv. phrase*

Activity A Write each sentence on your paper. Circle each prepositional phrase. Draw an arrow from the phrase to the word it describes.

Example On the sidewalk, a woman with a briefcase waits.

1. In the front yard of the house, the big dog growls.
2. The mother of the man appears on the porch of the house.
3. A short man in a black coat walks toward the door.
4. The big, old dog lies in the shade.
5. In the house, the young man visits with his mother.

When you write sentences with prepositional phrases, put each phrase where it makes the most sense.

Writing Tip

To express the meaning you want, place prepositional phrases as close as possible to the words they describe.

Activity B Read the facts. Decide which sentence makes more sense. Write the letter of the sentence that makes more sense on your paper.

1. **Facts** The bike has a horn. The bike is missing.

    A The bike with a horn is missing.

    B The bike is missing with a horn.

2. **Facts** The man had a dog. The man laughed at a joke.

    A The man laughed at a joke with the dog.

    B The man with the dog laughed at a joke.

Activity C Copy the following chart on your paper. Then read each sentence and fill in the chart. Like the example, some sentences have more than one prepositional phrase.

Example A runner with strong legs ran quickly around the track.

Phrase	Adj. or Adv.	Describes Which Word	Noun or Verb
with strong legs	adj.	runner	noun
around the track	adv.	ran	verb

1. Yesterday, a small, yellow airplane landed at the airport.
2. The young tiger leaps through the air in the jungle.
3. The dark blue car with large tires parked in the garage.
4. The runners with colored batons headed to the finish line.
5. The woman with the yellow shirt ran in the race.
6. The woman with the blue baton won the race.
7. The store on the corner opened during the weekend.
8. A duck with a yellow tail swam in the river.
9. A talented little girl sang in a concert at the park.
10. A friend of my mom's writes for a newspaper.

The runners with colored batons race around the track.

Common noun

The name of a general type of person, place, or thing

Proper noun

The name of a specific person, place, or thing

A **common noun** names a general type of person, place, or thing. A common noun does not begin with a capital letter.

Here are some common nouns.

EXAMPLE

state	woman	girl
man	city	boy

A **proper noun** names a specific person, place, or thing. A proper noun always begins with a capital letter.

EXAMPLE

Colorado	Aretha	Linda
Carlos	Seattle	Damon

Activity A Write this list of words on your paper. Use capital letters for proper nouns.

1. bird	**6.** dog	**11.** book	**16.** tree
2. justin	**7.** brenda	**12.** jackie	**17.** david
3. town	**8.** niagara falls	**13.** house	**18.** table
4. vancouver	**9.** tower	**14.** ontario	**19.** kim
5. park	**10.** cleveland	**15.** jeff	**20.** keiko

You have learned that a comma sets apart one or more words in a sentence. Use a comma after a prepositional phrase that begins a sentence.

EXAMPLE Under the porch, the dog lay in the mud.
(A comma follows the prepositional phrase *under the porch* to set it apart from the rest of the sentence.)

Activity B Write each sentence on your paper. Add a comma after the prepositional phrase that begins the sentence.

1. On the branch a bird perched.
2. In the hall friends chatted.
3. At the corner a car stopped.
4. Over the river a moose stood.
5. Beneath the water fish swim.

When writing sentences, remember to:

- Begin every sentence with a capital letter. End every sentence that makes a statement with a period.
- Begin proper nouns with capital letters.
- Do not begin common nouns with capital letters.
- Use a comma after a prepositional phrase that begins a sentence.

Activity C On your paper, write each sentence correctly with capital letters and commas. Put a period at the end of each sentence.

1. near the phone john waited silently
2. at the park karen skated
3. around the corner david talked with his friends
4. except for dwayne the members of the chorus sang
5. in the harbor the statue of liberty stands

The Statue of Liberty stands in New York Harbor.

Chapter 2 R E V I E W

Word Bank

adjective
prepositional
phrase

adverb
prepositional
phrase

common noun

object of the
preposition

preposition

prepositional
phrase

proper noun

state-of-being verb

Part A On a sheet of paper, write the correct word or words from the Word Bank to complete each sentence.

1. The name of a specific person, place, or thing is a _____.

2. A _____ is a word that ties or relates a noun or pronoun to another part of the sentence.

3. The noun or pronoun that follows the preposition is the _____ .

4. A _____ is a general type of person, place, or thing.

5. An _____ is a prepositional phrase that describes a verb.

6. A verb that does not show action is a _____ .

7. A _____ is a group of words that begins with a preposition and ends with a noun or pronoun.

8. A prepositional phrase that describes a noun is an ____.

Part B Add a different preposition to each phrase. Write each complete prepositional phrase on your paper.

9. _____ the tall building
10. _____ a distant corner
11. _____ the little house
12. _____ a late dinner

Part C Write each prepositional phrase on your paper. Tell whether it is an *adjective phrase* or an *adverb phrase*.

13. The dog with the long tail ran to me.

14. Melinda got off the bus.

15. I left my umbrella in your car.

Part D On your paper, write the letter of the simple subject of each sentence.

16. The students with good grades went to the park.
    A grades   B students   C went   D park

17. The school of fish swam down the stream.
    A school   B fish   C down   D stream

18. Everybody with a ticket can go into the theater now.
    A ticket   B theater   C Everybody   D now

Part E Read this paragraph about a race. Then answer the questions on your paper.

> The sleek cars with skillful drivers race around the track. A green flag waves. The cars roar past. A black car is ahead. The excited crowd jumps up.

19. Find these words in the story. Tell what part of speech each one is: *sleek, with, black, past, up, ahead, cars.*

20. Rewrite the first sentence so that it begins with a prepositional phrase. Remember to use a comma.

21. List all the verbs. There are five.

Part F Write each sentence on your paper. Underline each state-of-being verb. Circle each action verb.

22. I go to football games.   **24.** The game is over.

23. We cheer for our team.

Part G Write the words in bold on your paper. Then write whether each word is a *preposition* or an *adverb*.

25. Please sit **down.**

26. I live **down** the street.

Part H On your paper, write each sentence correctly with capital letters and commas. Don't forget the periods. Underline each preposition and circle each prepositional phrase.

27. after the race on friday people cheer for maria

28. jamal smiles at maria with pride

29. she talks about the olympics

30. maria is in the winner's circle

Test-Taking Tip Before answering questions about a paragraph, reread the parts of the paragraph that contain the information you need to answer each question correctly.

3 Using Compound Parts

Have you ever put together a puzzle together? When you first look at the tiny individual pieces, you might not be able to tell what the finished puzzle would look like. However, by matching and fitting together similar shapes and colors, you can eventually build the small pieces into a big picture that is complete and meaningful.

Sentences, like puzzles, are built of small parts that, when put together, have a larger meaning. In this chapter, you will study sentences with words that connect ideas.

Goals for Learning

◆ To introduce and use conjunctions

◆ To identify compound subjects, predicates, and objects of prepositions

◆ To combine two simple sentences to create a compound sentence

◆ To use commas and semicolons to punctuate sentences with compound parts

◆ To capitalize and punctuate titles correctly

Conjunction

A word that joins two or more words, phrases, or ideas in a sentence

A **conjunction** is a word that joins two or more words, phrases, or ideas in a sentence.

Here are some commonly used conjunctions:

and	but	yet
as well as	or	

EXAMPLE **Words** Larry and Anthony went to the store.
She's my friend as well as my cousin.

Phrases Did he go into the shop or down the sidewalk?

Ideas He travels around the country, yet he longs for the beach.
I tried hard, but I lost.

Activity A Write each sentence on your paper. Fill in the blank with a conjunction. Use *and, but, or, as well as,* or *yet.* More than one conjunction may make sense.

1. Tim _____ Lisa will call later.

2. The paper _____ the pencil are on the desk.

3. You should go to bed, _____ you will oversleep.

4. My sister _____ my mother arrived late.

5. The cat moved quickly _____ silently.

6. Cindy _____ Paul cleaned up.

7. His ancestors come from Spain _____ Portugal.

8. They traveled along wide city streets _____ narrow country roads.

9. A girl in running shorts _____ sneakers came to the door.

10. Slowly _____ violently, the storm swept through town.

Activity B Write each sentence on your paper. Circle the conjunction. Underline the words, phrases, or ideas that the conjunction connects in each sentence.

Examples Her <u>shoes</u>(and)<u>umbrella</u> are in the room.

We looked <u>in the closet</u>(as well as)<u>on the counter.</u>

<u>I arrived late,</u>(yet)<u>I sat up front.</u>

1. We spoke to Omar and Anita about the cleaning supplies.

2. Through the day and into the night, we worked.

3. Slowly but surely, the old house came to life.

4. Windows and floors sparkled.

5. The old yet sturdy house stood proudly.

These conjunctions come in sets, but they are separated in a sentence.

both—and	not only—but also
either—or	neither—nor

EXAMPLE   Both the snow and the icicles melted.
Either Maya or I will drive.
Not only Alvaro but also his dad left early.
Neither my keyboard nor my monitor worked.

Activity C On your paper, write a set of conjunctions for each sentence.

1. Unfortunately _____ her books _____ her homework were at school.

2. The books were _____ in her locker _____ in the classroom.

3. Ama studied _____ in the evening _____ in the morning before school.

4. Ama _____ rode to school _____ walked.

5. She _____ did well on her homework _____ passed a quiz.

A sentence may have more than one subject. A **compound subject** is two or more subjects joined by a conjunction.

Compound subject

Two or more subjects joined by a conjunction

EXAMPLE   Polar bears and reindeer live in the Arctic.

compound subject

(This sentence tells about two things that live in the Arctic—*polar bears* and *reindeer*. *Polar bears* and *reindeer* are two simple subjects that make up a compound subject when they are joined by the conjunction *and*. The complete subject is *polar bears and reindeer*.)

Compound subjects share a verb.

- Subjects joined by *and* take a plural verb.
- Singular subjects joined by *or* or *nor* take a singular verb.

Activity A Write the complete subject in these sentences on your paper. Underline the simple subjects in the compound subject. Circle the conjunction.

1. An alley and an empty store lie ahead.

2. Old products and dirty supplies sit on the shelves in the store.

3. Men and women clean during the cool morning.

4. The clean, empty street and store fill with shoppers.

5. The busy clerks and pleased shoppers smile at the change in the street.

When writing sentences with compound subjects, make sure the sentences are clear and easy for readers to understand.

Writing Tip

You can avoid repeating words by combining the subjects of two or more short sentences into a compound subject. Creating a compound subject can make your writing better.

EXAMPLE   Red tomatoes, purple grapes, yellow melons, and green beans are on sale.
(*Tomatoes, grapes, melons,* and *beans* are the simple subjects in the compound subject.)

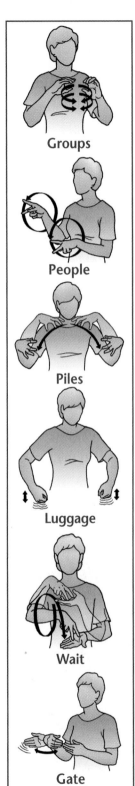

Groups

People

Piles

Luggage

Wait

Gate

Activity B Write the compound subject for each sentence. Underline each simple subject. Circle the conjunction.

1. A duck, a chicken, and a spotted pig stood in the yard.

2. A taxi, a bus, and an old truck drove around the block.

3. A tall lamp, a round table, and a large bed sat in the store window.

4. Kimi, Dawn, and Deepa step into the airplane.

5. Groups of people and piles of luggage wait at the gate.

You can often combine the subjects of two or more sentences into a compound subject and make the two sentences into one sentence.

EXAMPLE	Brandon talked. Hannah talked.
	Brandon and Hannah talked.
	Lakes can freeze. Rivers can freeze.
	Lakes and rivers can freeze.

Activity C Write each pair of sentences as one sentence with a compound subject.

1. Chris went to the movies. Marco went to the movies.

2. A tape played loudly. A CD played loudly.

3. The old table broke. The old chair broke.

4. The moon shone brightly. The stars shone brightly.

5. Ted works at the bank. Trish works at the bank.

Groups of people and piles of luggage wait at the gate.

Compound predicate

Two or more verbs joined by a conjunction

A sentence may have more than one predicate. A **compound predicate** is two or more verbs joined by a conjunction.

EXAMPLE The plastic melted and stuck to the table.

compound predicate

(This sentence tells about two things that the plastic did—*melted* and *stuck. Melted* and *stuck* form a compound predicate made up of two simple predicates, or verbs. They are joined by the conjunction *and.* The complete predicate is *melted and stuck to the table.*)

Activity A Write the complete predicate in these sentences on your paper. Underline the verbs in the compound predicate. Circle the conjunction.

1. A long train whistles and eases around the curve.
2. Tracks bend and groan under the weight of the train.
3. The slow train rattles and squeaks along the tracks.
4. Clouds of dust from the train rise and settle on the road.
5. The long train sways and fades into the distance.

Railroad cars are linked together. Conjunctions link the verbs of a compound predicate.

A conjunction may join two or more verbs in the predicate.

EXAMPLE The crowd yelled, jumped, and cheered.
(*Yelled, jumped,* and *cheered* are the verbs in the compound predicate.)

Activity B Write the complete predicate for each sentence. Underline each simple predicate. Circle the conjunction.

1. Joe sits in the new car, drives along the street, and honks at friends.

2. The young man looks for a store, stops, parks, and walks down the street.

3. Joe goes into the store, looks at the shelves, and talks to the owner.

4. The young buyer laughs, jokes, and pays for a CD.

5. Joe gets into his car, roars past the park, and turns onto the highway.

You can often combine the predicates of two or more sentences into a compound predicate and make the two sentences into one sentence.

EXAMPLE Amanda sat. Amanda groaned.
Amanda sat and groaned.
Ichiro made lunch. Ichiro sat at the counter.
Ichiro made lunch and sat at the counter.

Activity C Write each pair of sentences as one sentence with a compound predicate.

1. Mark ate at the counter. Mark drank at the counter.

2. Sue watched television. Sue went to bed.

3. The old dog barked. The old dog howled.

4. The brown rabbit jumped. The brown rabbit ran away.

5. The women sat at the table. The women talked at the table.

Compound object of preposition

Two or more objects of one preposition joined by a conjunction

Some sentences with compound subjects may also have adjective prepositional phrases. The object of a prepositional phrase may be compound, too.

EXAMPLE   The man in the jacket and scarf and the boy with the bicycle spoke softly.
Compound subject   man and boy
Compound object of a preposition   jacket and scarf

It may seem difficult at first to locate the simple subjects in a sentence with a compound subject, prepositional phrases, and **compound objects of the preposition.** However, there are some steps you can follow to find the subjects.

1. Find the verb.

2. Ask who or what is doing the action. (The answer is more than one word if the subject is compound.)

3. Find the prepositions. Remember that the object of a preposition is never the subject.

Activity A Write this sentence on your paper. Then follow the directions.

The salad with oranges and nuts and the frozen yogurt in the pint container sat in the sun.

1. Draw a line under the simple predicate.

2. Draw two lines under the complete subject.

3. Write the simple subjects found in the compound subject. Circle the conjunction.

4. Put brackets [ ] around the prepositional phrases in the complete subject.

5. Circle the object or compound object of each preposition in the complete subject.

Activity B On your paper, write the simple subjects that make up the compound subject of each sentence.

1. Diane in a white sweater and Rosa in a blue coat wait outside a theater in the cool breeze.

2. The girls and a few other friends talk about the new movie and the actors.

3. Behind the girls, more men, women, and teenagers crowd onto the sidewalk and the street.

4. At the curb, a man in a dark suit and a woman in a pink dress arrive.

5. The girls and the large crowd of men and women cheer for the famous couple.

Activity C Write each sentence on your paper. Circle each preposition and underline each object of the preposition.

1. A yellow plane with a number on the wing and a silver plane with a blue design bounce along the rough ground.

2. The model plane with red and green lights glides high above the trees.

3. A wooden plane and a metal plane wait with their owners in the open field of short grass.

4. People with video cameras and reporters with microphones watch carefully.

5. The silver and blue plane flies high, soars above the trees, and wins easily.

The compound parts of sentences have similarities and differences like these two planes.

Compound Sentence

A sentence made up of two or more complete sentences joined by a conjunction

A **compound sentence** is two or more sentences joined by a conjunction. A compound sentence joins two related ideas. Each part of a compound sentence has a subject and a verb.

 EXAMPLE

Sentence	The football player ran onto the field.
	↓ ↓
Sentence parts	subject verb
Sentence	The fans rose from their seats.
	↓ ↓
Sentence parts	subject verb

Sentence parts	subject verb
	↓ ↓
Compound sentence	The football player ran onto the field, and the fans rose from their seats.
	↓ ↓
Sentence parts	subject verb

(In the compound sentence, the two related ideas are joined by the conjunction *and*. A comma is used before the conjunction to separate the two parts of the compound sentence.)

Writing Tip

Using compound sentences helps you write more ideas in each sentence. This helps you include more information and gives your writing variety.

Activity A Write the sentences on your paper. Underline the two complete ideas. Circle the conjunction.

Example <u>The day was long,</u> (and) <u>the competition was tough</u>.

1. The winning car rolls across the finish line, and the driver smiles with joy.

2. In the stands, a friend cheers, and a brother grins.

3. The driver waves, and the crowd yells louder.

4. On the track, a black car crosses over the line, and a red car limps into the pit.

5. The race is done, and the race crews pack up all of their tools.

Rain

Happen, Occur

But

Ground

Dry

Stay

Activity B Write the subjects and verbs in these sentences on your paper. Write the conjunction that joins the sentence parts.

Example   The rain falls, but the ground stays dry.

Subjects	rain, ground
Verbs	falls, stays
Conjunction	but

1. The man works on a puzzle, and the woman reads silently in the big chair.

2. The couple sits quietly, and the rain splashes against the window.

3. During the storm, the radio crackles, and the lights dim.

4. The long day passes, and darkness falls swiftly.

5. The power fails, but the couple sits by the fire.

Activity C Combine each pair of sentences into a compound sentence. Use the conjunction in parentheses. Don't forget to put a comma before the conjunction.

Example   A dog barked in the distance.

Michael huddled in the corner. (and)

A dog barked in the distance, and Michael huddled in the corner.

1. Shadows moved across the wall. The door creaked softly. (and)

2. Michael sat up. The noise faded away. (but)

3. The wind died down. Michael tossed and turned. (yet)

4. The sun came up. The day began. (and)

5. Michael was tired. He went to school. (but)

The rain falls, but the ground stays dry.

Compound

Two or more words, phrases, or ideas joined by a conjunction

You have learned about compound subjects, compound predicates, compound objects of a preposition, and compound sentences.

Compounds are two or more words, phrases, or ideas joined by a conjunction. Some sentences have one compound part. Some sentences have two or more compound parts.

Activity A On your paper, write each sentence. Fill in the missing compound shown in parentheses.

1. Nurses watched over the patients during the day and
   _____ . (object of the preposition)

2. The _____ and men walked toward the bus stop.
   (subject)

3. The bus driver _____ and looked at the train crossing.
   (verb)

4. Alice and _____ waited for Belinda. (subject)

5. Belinda laughed and _____ to her friends. (verb)

Activity B Write the compounds found in each of these sentences. Write the kind of compound used.

Example   A team of workers and volunteers drove steadily through the morning.

            workers and volunteers—objects of the preposition

1. Alberto parked and sat on the pier with his fishing pole.

2. The window fan in the diner blew through the grease and smoke.

3. Crisp, green salads and long pans of tasty meats sat on the table.

4. The angler with a pole, boat, and motor fished in the middle of the river.

5. A car and a motor home turned into the park.

Activity C Read each sentence. On your paper, write the compound part of each sentence. Then write whether it is a *compound subject,* a *compound predicate,* a *compound object of a preposition,* or a *compound sentence.*

1. A gray cat climbed out through a window, and then he ran across the yard.

2. He jumped over the bushes and fence.

3. A small, red car braked and skidded to a sudden stop.

4. The cat jumped through the window of the car, and the driver screamed in fright.

5. The driver and a woman passenger in the car looked for the owner of the cat.

Activity D Read the paragraph. Then write the answer to each item on your paper.

> The fish pulled on the hook and line. The fishing rod bent, and the reel buzzed. The angler and the fish pulled hard. The angler bent and reached toward the fish. The smart fish scraped against a rock under the water. The angler stood up, and the fish splashed. Then the rain and wind picked up. Not only the angler but also the fish headed for home and safety.

1. Write the sentence that has no compounds.

2. What kind of compound does the first sentence have?

3. Write one of the two sentences that has a compound subject but no other compound parts. Underline the simple subjects.

4. Write the sentence that has a compound predicate. Underline the verbs.

5. Write one of the two compound sentences. Underline the two ideas. Circle the conjunction.

Semicolon (;)

A punctuation mark that separates two related ideas not connected by a conjunction

Use commas in sentences with three or more compound parts.

EXAMPLE

Cats often meow, purr, scratch, or hiss.

Parts of speech	noun	adv.	verb	verb	verb	conj.	verb

Sentence parts   subject I compound predicate

Activity A   On your paper, write each sentence. Add commas, capital letters, and periods.

Communication Connection

Today more people than ever use e-mail to communicate with others. Some experts predict that by the year 2005 people will send more than 36 billion e-mail messages per day.

1. carrots corn tomatoes beans and peas grow in the garden
2. spiders flies and mice wait in the basement
3. people eat sleep and rise again for another day
4. swings slides and monkey bars sat on the empty playground
5. cheerleaders bend jump dance and yell
6. toys books and clothes lie on the floor
7. bears snakes and monkeys live in the zoo
8. smoke sparks and flames pour from the chimney
9. I sent an e-mail to the coach the teacher and the principal
10. Computers TVs and keyboards are in that room

You have learned to use commas in compound sentences. Place a comma after the first complete idea, just before the conjunction. You can use a **semicolon** instead of a conjunction to separate two related ideas in a sentence.

EXAMPLE   Some people sing, but other people dance.
Some people sing; other people dance.

Quotation marks ("")

Punctuation used around the title of a part of a large work

Underline the titles of books, magazines, newspapers, and CDs when writing by hand.

Using What You've Learned

Imagine that you have recently read a magazine article about a CD that you like. Write a letter to a friend, telling about the article. In your letter, include the name of the magazine, the article, and the CD. Remember to write the titles correctly.

Activity B On your paper, write each pair of sentences as one compound sentence. Use a comma with a conjunction in three of the sentences. Use a semicolon in the other two.

1. Skaters glide. Bicyclists ride.

2. The night wind blew. The moon disappeared.

3. Dinner burned in the oven. The smoke alarm rang.

4. The sun shone. People headed toward the beach.

5. Time passed. Night fell.

You know that a proper noun begins with a capital letter. Titles are proper nouns. Titles begin with capital letters.

Titles of books appear in *italic* (or underlined). The same is true for the titles of magazines, newspapers, and CDs. Each is a complete work. Parts of works such as chapters, articles, and songs need **quotation marks** around them. Remember:

- The title of a large work should be printed in italic (or underlined).

- The title of a part of a large work should be in quotation marks.

EXAMPLE The book is <u>World of Architecture.</u>
The book is *World of Architecture.*
The chapter is "Modern Buildings."

Activity C On your paper, correct each sentence. Use capital letters and periods. Underline titles of whole works. Use quotation marks around parts of works.

1. the newspaper is the daily news and information

2. the CD is songs of jazz; the song is a jazz evening

3. the book is canada cooking; the chapter is cooking chicken

4. the book is fix your car; the chapter is spark plugs

5. the magazine is surf and stuff; the article is surfing clubs

Chapter 3   R E V I E W

Word Bank

compound

compound object
of preposition

compound
predicate

compound
sentence

compound subject

conjunction

quotation marks

semicolon

Part A Read each sentence below. Fill in each blank with a vocabulary word that correctly completes the sentence.

1. A _____ is two or more subjects joined by a conjunction.
2. Place _____ around the title of part of a large work.
3. Two or more words, phrases, or ideas joined by a conjunction is a _____.
4. You can create a _____ by combining two or more complete sentences with a conjunction.
5. A _____ is two or more objects of one preposition joined by a conjunction.
6. Two or more predicates joined by a conjunction is a _____.
7. A _____ joins two or more words, phrase, or ideas.
8. Use a _____ to separate two related ideas not connected by a conjunction.

Part B Read the sentences. Write the conjunctions and the words they connect on your paper.

9. Janet and Maria spent the day at the fair.
10. They ate hot dogs and popcorn and then went to the rides.
11. The roller coaster was noisy, but it was the most fun.
12. Neither Janet nor Maria was scared in the haunted house.

Part C Write each pair of sentences as a single sentence. Use conjunctions to connect subjects, verbs, or objects of prepositions. Underline any compound subjects, predicates, and objects of prepositions.

13. Whitney pulls over in the car. She shouts to her friends.
14. Irena sings beautifully. Irena dances beautifully.
15. A woman with a briefcase got on the bus. A boy in a football uniform got on the bus.
16. Juan went to the store. Juan went to the gym.
17. Gerald likes to read. Lisa likes to read.

Part D Read each sentence. Then answer the questions that follow. Write the letter of the sentences.

> **A** A man and a woman with a large trunk and a small box wait on a dusty bench inside the station.
> **B** At the station, the man and the woman climb into the train and sit down near a window.
> **C** The whistle blows, and the train moves.

18. Which sentence has a compound verb?

19. Which sentence has a compound object of a preposition?

20. Which sentence is a compound sentence?

Part E Write each pair of sentences as one compound sentence. Use a semicolon in one of the sentences.

21. The car stopped. The driver fixed the flat tire.

22. The team practiced. Reporters watched.

Part F Choose the correct way to write each underlined item.

23. The newspaper called <u>usa news</u> is on the table.
   A USA news   **C** *Usa News*
   B *USA News*   **D** "USA News"

24. The book has a chapter titled <u>the right machine.</u>
   A "the right machine."   **C** *The Right Machine.*
   B The Right Machine.   **D** "The Right Machine."

25. Find a recipe in the book <u>joys of grilling.</u>
   A *Joys of Grilling.*   **C** Joys of Grilling.
   B "joys of grilling."   **D** "Joys of Grilling."

Test-Taking Tip If you know you will have to define terms on a test, write the term on one side of a card. Write its definition on the other side. Use the cards to test yourself.

4 Direct Objects

Have you ever watched an exciting soccer game? When you are watching a good game, it is sometimes hard to find the player who has the ball. You try to follow the ball from player to player. One player passes the ball. Another player kicks the ball. The forward passes the ball to a teammate. Sometimes a goalkeeper blocks the ball. The ball receives most of the action.

In this chapter, you will study words that take the action of the verb.

Goals for Learning

◆ To identify the *subject + verb + direct object* sentence pattern

◆ To identify simple and compound direct objects

◆ To use pronouns correctly in place of nouns

◆ To capitalize titles of people and abstract proper nouns

◆ To punctuate compound sentences correctly

Direct object

A noun or pronoun that receives action directly from the verb

In earlier lessons, you focused on one sentence pattern: *subject + verb.* Now you will learn about a second sentence pattern: *subject + verb + direct object.*

A **direct object** is a noun or pronoun that receives action directly from the verb.

EXAMPLE   Yoshi watched.

Sentence pattern   subject | verb
Yoshi watched the clock.

Sentence pattern   subject + verb + direct object
(The noun *clock* receives the action of the verb *watched.*
Yoshi watched *what?* Yoshi watched the *clock. Clock* is the direct object.)

Here are more examples of sentences with action verbs and direct objects. Notice that in each sentence the noun receives action directly from the verb.

EXAMPLE   Lynda mailed the **letter.**

Sentence pattern   subject + verb + direct object
(Lynda mailed *what?* Lynda mailed the *letter. Letter* is the direct object.)

                        The friends ate **lunch.**
(The friends ate *what?* The friends ate *lunch. Lunch* is the direct object.)

A direct object helps complete a thought in a sentence. To find the direct object, ask *what* or *whom.* Then look for the word or words that answer the question.

Activity A On your paper, write each sentence. Draw an arrow from the bold verb to the direct object.

Example   The ball **hits** the net.

1. A farmer **watches** the rain.

2. The water **washes** the corn.

3. The rain **forms** a puddle.

4. The ground **swallows** the water.

5. The plant roots **drink** the water.

Lunch

Friend

Eat

Finish

The friends
ate lunch.

Activity B Fill in the blank with a direct object. Write the completed sentences on your paper.

1. Jim opened the _____ .

2. The bat hit the _____ .

3. Bright sunlight lit the _____ .

4. A sharp saw cut the _____ .

5. The cat caught a _____ .

Adjectives can describe nouns that are direct objects.

> **EXAMPLE**
>
> The girls watched an old TV show.
>
> | | | | | | |
>
> **Parts of speech**   *adj. noun   verb   adj. adj. adj. noun*
> **Sentence pattern**   subject + verb + direct object
> (The adjectives *an, old,* and *TV* describe the direct object *show.*)

Activity C Write the sentences on your paper. Circle the direct object. Do not include adjectives. Draw an arrow from the verb to the direct object. The verb is in bold.

Example   Thick clouds **surrounded** the quiet (city.)

1. A scientist **pushed** two buttons.

2. Sparks **filled** the cold, dreary room.

3. The scientist **created** a giant monster.

4. The scientist **watched** his creation.

5. The monster **opened** the heavy steel door.

Activity D Write each sentence. Label the subject (*s.*), the verb (*v.*), and the direct object (*d. obj.*).

1. The farmer plowed the muddy field.

2. Ronald hit a long fly ball.

3. Sarah brought an old green book.

4. A brown squirrel climbed a tall oak tree.

5. The shivering boy closed the kitchen window.

Direct objects can be compound. Two or more direct objects joined by a conjunction make a **compound direct object**.

Compound direct object

Two or more direct objects joined by a conjunction

EXAMPLE

The seamstress sewed the dress and the veil.

Parts of speech adj. noun verb adj. noun conj. adj. noun
Sentence pattern subject + verb + direct object
(The two nouns *dress* and *veil* receive the action of the verb *sewed*. The seamstress sewed *what?* The seamstress sewed the dress and veil. The nouns *dress* and *veil* make up the compound direct object. They are joined by the conjunction *and*.)

Activity A On your paper, write the compound direct object in each sentence. Do not include adjectives.

Example Winter brings ice and heavy snow.
          compound direct object—ice, snow

1. The big storm floods streets and homes.

2. Water fills basements and yards.

3. Big tree limbs block the sidewalks and streets.

4. Cara watches the muddy water and floating branches.

5. A warm sun slowly dries the puddles and mud.

Two sentences with direct objects can be joined to form a compound sentence. Both ideas in the compound sentence will have direct objects.

EXAMPLE

Marina ordered a salad.
Todd got spaghetti.

Compound sentence Marina ordered salad, and Todd got spaghetti.

(Each part of the compound sentence has a direct object. Marina ordered *what?* She ordered a salad. *Salad* is the direct object of the verb *ordered*. Todd got *what?* He got spaghetti. *Spaghetti* is the direct object of the verb *got*. The two ideas are joined by the conjunction *and*.)

Activity B Write these compound sentences on your paper. Circle the direct object of each verb. The verbs are in bold.

Example Aman and Tony **wrote** poor (paragraphs), but they **wanted** good (grades).

1. Aman **reads** science fiction stories, but Tony **chooses** war stories.

2. Rosa **played** the piano, and Amy **read** a book.

3. One **likes** music, but the other **likes** books.

4. Rosa **played** loud music, and Amy **covered** her ears.

5. Amy **left** the room, and Rosa **pounded** on the piano keys.

The direct object follows the verb in a sentence. The direct object is always part of the complete predicate.

EXAMPLE
The class heard the important news yesterday.

Sentence parts   complete subject | complete predicate
Sentence pattern   subject + verb + direct object
(The complete predicate includes the verb *heard* plus the direct object *news* and its adjectives *the* and *important*. The adverb *yesterday* answers the question *when* about the verb. *Yesterday* is also part of the complete predicate.)

Activity C Write each sentence on your paper. Draw one line under the complete subject. Draw two lines under the complete predicate. Draw a circle around the direct object or compound direct object.

Example The TV news and the highway patrol warned (people) about a heavy flood.

1. Men, women, and children left the area in their cars.

2. The storm hit the coast and harbors suddenly.

3. The high waves rocked and damaged the boats.

4. Waves and strong winds sank one boat.

5. Thunder and lightning split the sky.

A sentence can have a compound subject, a compound verb, and a compound direct object. Do not confuse compound sentences with sentences that have compound parts. Remember, a compound sentence has two complete ideas joined by a conjunction.

EXAMPLE   Fireworks and rockets thrill and excite families and friends.

Compound subject	Fireworks and rockets
Compound verb	thrill and excite
Compound direct object	families and friends

(Although the sentence has compound parts, it does not have two ideas joined by a conjunction. It is not a compound sentence.)

Compound sentence	Fireworks and rockets thrill the crowd, **but** only some fireworks excite small children and their friends.

(This sentence is a compound sentence because it has two ideas joined by the conjunction *but*. The first part of the sentence has the compound subject *fireworks* and *rockets*. The second part of the sentence has the compound direct object *children* and *friends*.)

Activity A Number your paper from 1 to 5. Read each sentence. Decide whether it is a compound sentence. If it is compound, write *C*. If it is not compound, write *NC*.

1. Cats and dogs scratch and tear rugs and chairs.

2. Maria mowed the lawn, and Joe trimmed the hedge.

3. David and Mark washed and waxed the car and the truck.

4. The driver emptied the trunk, and his friend carried the boxes and bags inside.

5. The farmer and his son fed the pigs and cows, and their guest fed the horses.

In sentences that have compound verbs, each verb may have its own direct object.

EXAMPLE Jason made breakfast and cleaned the pots.

Compound verb made and cleaned
(*Breakfast* is the direct object of *made*. *Pots* is the direct object of *cleaned*.)

In sentences that have compound verbs, each verb may have a compound direct object.

EXAMPLE Chris washed the sheets and towels and ironed the shirts and dresses.

Compound verb washed and ironed
(The compound direct object of *washed* is *sheets* and *towels*. The compound direct object of *ironed* is *shirts* and *dresses*.)

Activity B Number your paper from 1 to 5. Write whether the sentence has a *compound verb,* a *compound direct object,* or *both.*

1. Ben ordered pancakes and eggs.

2. Kim drank coffee and read the morning paper.

3. A server brought the pancakes and poured coffee and juice.

4. Along with his waffle, Eddie wanted strawberries and cream.

5. Ben finished breakfast and left the diner.

Activity C On your paper, write whether the sentence has a *compound subject,* a *compound verb,* or a *compound direct object.* If the sentence is a compound sentence, write *CS.*

1. The birds chirped tunes, and the squirrels gathered nuts.

2. A rabbit ate carrots and lettuce in the garden.

3. The boy and his sister caught fish for dinner.

4. The player removed his hat and glove.

5. Gerri washed the car and tuned the engine.

Direct objects can have prepositional phrases.

EXAMPLE The juice stained the dress with pink roses.

Sentence pattern subject + verb + direct object + adjective prepositional phrase

(The adjective prepositional phrase *with pink roses* describes the noun *dress,* the direct object.)

Activity A Write each sentence on your paper. Underline the direct object. Circle the prepositional phrase that tells about the direct object.

Example Brady read a <u>book</u>(about a detective).

1. A fire burned a tall building of offices.

2. Workers carried boxes of papers.

3. Firefighters sprayed water from a nearby hydrant.

4. Flames burned the walls inside the building.

5. A brave woman saved a man with a broken leg.

A prepositional phrase that follows a direct object may describe the direct object, or it may describe the verb. Some sentences may have prepositional phrases that describe the direct object *and* prepositional phrases that describe the verb.

EXAMPLE The camper carries a bag with snacks.

(The adjective phrase *with snacks* describes the direct object *bag.* It tells which bag.)

The camper carries a bag on her back.

(The adverb phrase *on her back* tells about the verb *carries.* It tells where the camper carries the bag.)

The camper carries a bag with snacks on her back.

(The adjective phrase *with snacks* describes the direct object *bag.* The adverb phrase *on her back* tells about the verb *carries.*)

Activity B Write each sentence on your paper. Circle each prepositional phrase. Draw an arrow from each phrase to the word it describes.

Example   The driver grabbed the wheel (of the car) (with his left hand).

1. The horse threw the rider during the rodeo.

2. The crowd cheered the brave rider on the ground.

3. The horse jumped the fence near the side gate.

4. The rider wiped the dust on his pants with his scarf.

5. Josie met a group of friends after the rodeo.

Activity C On your paper, make a chart of the prepositional phrases in these sentences. Write the type of prepositional phrase.

Example   The girl with the hat pulled the boat with green sails toward the shore.

Prepositional Phrases	Adjective or Adverb?
with the hat	adjective
with green sails	adjective
toward the shore	adverb

1. The smart fish twisted the line of heavy nylon around a rock.

2. The man in the boat grabbed the line near the surface.

3. The fish pulled the angler with his gear from the boat.

4. A friend in another boat offered help to the man in the water.

5. The angler thanked his friend on the boat for rescuing him.

Saddle bronc riding was a popular activity long before rodeo became a sport.

You have learned that nouns can appear in three places in sentences. A noun can be any of the following:

- the subject of a sentence
- the direct object of a sentence
- the object of a preposition

Some sentences have nouns in all three places.

> **EXAMPLE**   The woman hung the pants in her closet.
> | | |
>   subject   direct obj.   obj. of prep.

Activity A Write each noun in the following sentences on your paper. Next to each noun, write whether it is the *subject, direct object,* or *object of preposition* (Remember that nouns name persons, places, and things.)

1. The sleek car squealed away from the curb onto the freeway.
2. Craig hit third gear, and the engine howled.
3. A squirrel jumped off the road, away from the car.
4. The gauge on the dash showed an almost empty tank of gas.
5. Craig walked away from the car toward a gas station down the road.
6. People on the ship watched the lights of the city by the harbor.
7. The ship left the harbor and sailed toward the sea.
8. Lightning split the sky, and rain drenched the ship.
9. During the storm, a lamp fell from the table in a shower of sparks.
10. The captain steered the ship to another safe harbor.

Many things that nouns name we can see and touch, such as *store*, *book*, and *dog*. Some things we cannot see or touch, such as *dream*, *idea*, and *time*. A **concrete noun** names something that we can see or touch. An **abstract noun** names something that we cannot see or touch. Here are some examples.

Concrete Nouns	Abstract Nouns
flame	warmth
tree	thirst
pen	truth
ball	action
camera	love

Concrete nouns are things you know about through your senses (sight, hearing, touch, taste, or smell). Abstract nouns name ideas, qualities, feelings, or characteristics.

How can you be sure a word is a noun? Remember that articles (*a*, *an*, and *the*) point out common nouns. If you can use an article with it, the word is a noun.

Activity B Write each noun in these sentences on your paper. Tell whether it is *concrete* or *abstract*.

1. Chuck had a dream about a horse.
2. The heat from the fire warmed the campers.
3. The bell on the wall made a sound.
4. Anita took time off from work.
5. Tom saw hunger in the eyes of the kitten.
6. Kisha liked the action and excitement of football.
7. Light from the TV filled the room.
8. Karen had an idea for a game.
9. Bill saw love in the eyes of the old dog.
10. The video filled Joe with fear.

A **pronoun** is a word that replaces a noun in a sentence.

Pronoun
A word that takes the place of a noun

Nominative pronoun

A pronoun used as the subject of a sentence

Objective pronoun

A pronoun that is the direct object or object of the preposition

> **EXAMPLE**
>
> Food spoils quickly in the heat.
> It spoils quickly in the heat.
>
> Sentence parts   subject | predicate
> Sentence pattern   subject + verb
>
> (*Food* is a noun. *It* is a pronoun. In the second sentence, the pronoun *it* replaces the noun *food*.)

Pronouns have different forms, or cases.

Pronouns		
	Nominative	**Objective**
One		
First person	I	me
Second person	you	you
Third person	he, she, it	him, her, it
Two or More		
First person	we	us
Second person	you	you
Third person	they	them

A **nominative pronoun** replaces a noun that is the subject of a sentence.

> **EXAMPLE**
>
> Rosalia celebrated Thanksgiving with her cousins.
> She celebrated Thanksgiving with her cousins.

An **objective pronoun** replaces a noun that is the direct object or object of the preposition.

> **EXAMPLE**
>
> Rosalia celebrated Thanksgiving with her cousins.
> Rosalia celebrated it with her cousins.
> Rosalia celebrated Thanksgiving with her cousins.
> Rosalia celebrated Thanksgiving with them.

Writing Tip

Pronouns connected by the verb *be* should be in the same case. *It is me* sounds right because that is what people usually say. But *It is I* is correct.

We can use more than one pronoun in a sentence.

EXAMPLE   She brought it for him.

Activity A For each sentence, choose the correct pronoun. Write the pronoun on your paper, and tell what part of the sentence it is.

Example   (We, Us) heard the bird sing.

          We—subject

1. (She, Her) looked through the window and saw (they, them) in the rain.

2. Quickly, (I, me) opened the door for (they, them).

3. (He, Him) waited for (we, us) at home.

4. The roof leaked water on (they, them) and dropped plaster on (she, her) and (I, me).

5. (We, Us) left the house, and dark storm clouds dumped rain on (we, us).

6. (We, Us) and (they, them) ran to the bus.

7. The bus dropped some of (they, them) off at the corner.

8. (We, Us) rode with (she, her) to another street.

9. The bus left (he, him) and (we, us) on the curb.

10. Then (he, him) and (I, me) walked through the rain to a shelter with (she, her).

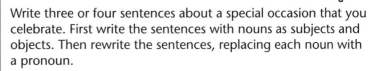

Using What You've Learned

Write three or four sentences about a special occasion that you celebrate. First write the sentences with nouns as subjects and objects. Then rewrite the sentences, replacing each noun with a pronoun.

Pronouns help you avoid repeating the same nouns over and over again. They help your sentences sound better.

EXAMPLE   Yoshi and Malcolm went for a walk Saturday morning. Suddenly, Yoshi and Malcolm spotted a rabbit in the street. Yoshi and Malcolm stopped and watched the rabbit.

Yoshi and Malcolm went for a walk Saturday morning. Suddenly, they spotted a rabbit in the street. They stopped and watched it.

(In the second group of sentences, pronouns replace the repeated nouns. The pronouns make the sentences sound more like natural speech.)

Do not use pronouns unless readers will know exactly which noun the pronoun is replacing. Sometimes, for clarity, it may be better to repeat the noun.

EXAMPLE   Juan met Paulo at the library. He worked there. (*Who* worked at the library? Did Juan or Paulo work at the library? In this case, the pronoun makes the meaning of the sentence unclear. It would have been better to repeat the noun *Paulo*.)

Activity A Write each sentence on your paper. Change the words in bold to pronouns. Be sure to use the correct form for each pronoun. Look at the table in Lesson 6 on page 78 for help.

1. **Josh and Andrea** walked into the busy store and saw Maria and Carlos.

2. Josh signed "hello" to **Maria and Carlos.**

3. **Maria** bought a loaf of bread.

4. Carlos talked to **Andrea** about the soccer game.

5. The clerk filled the bag and gave **the bag** to Carlos.

Communication Connection

One out of every thousand people is born deaf. More than one-third of the U.S. population has a hearing problem by age 65.

Some pronouns end with *-self* or *-selves.*

myself	herself	ourselves
yourself	yourselves	itself
himself	themselves	

Activity B Write each sentence on your paper. Fill in the blank with the correct *-self* pronoun.

1. I did it by _____ .

2. He did it by _____ .

3. You did it by _____ .

4. They did it by _____ .

5. We did it by _____ .

Some pronouns refer to things and people in general. No specific person or thing is pointed out.

Pronouns that do not refer to specific people or things are indefinite pronouns. *Indefinite* means "not defined or specific."

People		Things
someone	somebody	something
anyone	anybody	anything
everyone	everybody	everything
no one	nobody	nothing

Activity C Write each pronoun in these sentences on your paper. Write whether the pronoun is a *subject,* a *direct object,* or an *object of a preposition.*

1. In a small town, everyone knows everything about everybody.

2. In a big city, hardly anyone knows anything about anybody.

3. Someone knows everything about somebody.

4. Everyone knows something about somebody.

5. Everyone knows something about nothing.

Lesson **8** Pronoun or Adjective?

Some words in the English language can be more than one part of speech.

These words can be pronouns or adjectives.

all	few	other
another	many	several
any	one (or any other number)	some
each		

EXAMPLE   **Adjective**   Some snow melted.
              Pronoun   Some melted.

(In the first sentence, *some* is an adjective that describes the noun subject *snow.* In the second sentence, *some* is a pronoun that takes the place of the noun subject *snow. Some* is the subject of the sentence.)

Some pronouns are two words.

each other	one another

EXAMPLE   Claudia and Brittany see each other every week.
              Claudia, Brittany, and Fiona see one another.

Activity A On your paper, write each adjective and the noun it describes.

1. Many people work two jobs.

2. Some men work at several jobs.

3. Each person tries all kinds of jobs.

4. One woman tried ten jobs.

5. Another woman wanted any job.

Activity B On your paper, copy each word in bold. Then tell whether it is an *adjective* or a *pronoun*.

1. **Some** people like football games.
2. I like a **few** of them.
3. Sarah likes **some** kinds of sports.
4. She saw **two** games in the fall.
5. Good players on a team play well and share the glory with **one another.**

Activity C On your paper, use each of these terms as a pronoun in a sentence.

1. each other
2. ten
3. anybody
4. several
5. everybody
6. another
7. one another
8. each
9. nothing
10. some

Activity D On your paper, use each of these words as an adjective in a sentence.

1. ten
2. several
3. another
4. each
5. some

Some college football stadiums have room for over 100,000 fans.

This, that, these, and *those* can be more than one part of speech. They can be either pronouns or adjectives.

> **EXAMPLE** **Adjective** That water boiled on the stove.
> **Pronoun** That boiled on the stove.
>
> (In the first sentence, *that* is an adjective that describes the noun subject *water.* In the second sentence, *that* is a pronoun that takes the place of the noun subject *water. That* is the subject of the sentence.)

Activity A On your paper, write the adjective that describes each noun in bold.

1. These **stores** have many items for sale.

2. That **music box** plays a tune.

3. This **mirror** shines brightly in that **light.**

4. That **watch** keeps good time.

5. Those **lamps** go nicely with that **table.**

Activity B Copy each word in bold on your paper. Then write whether it is an *adjective* or a *pronoun.*

1. **That** book dropped to the floor.

2. I want **this.**

3. **These** belong on the shelf.

4. Tim will wrap **those** packages for you.

5. Julio lost **that** on the bus.

6. Ali caught **this** fish by herself.

7. **This** matches **that** jacket.

8. **Those** flowers look nice.

9. Nina sat on **that** chair.

10. **That** stands along the wall.

This, that, these, and *those* point out persons and things.

The word *this* points out one person or thing that is near. The word *that* points out one person or thing that is in the distance.

This boy beside me won the contest.
That girl by the tree entered the contest.

The word *these* points out more than one person or thing that is near. The word *those* points out more than one person or thing that is in the distance.

These workers over here served the meal.
Those workers near the sink cleaned up.

Activity C Write each sentence on your paper. Fill in the blank with *This, That, These,* or *Those.*

Example   Thing: mirror near you
    __This__ hangs on the wall.

1. Thing: vase across the room
    _____ sits on the table.

2. Thing: rug near you
    _____ lies on the floor.

3. Thing: tall plants across the room
    _____ stand in the corner.

4. Thing: curtains near you
    _____ hang at the window.

5. Thing: clock near you
    _____ goes on the shelf.

Lesson 10 | Writing Mechanics

Capitalize
To use capital letters

Proper nouns can be examples of abstract nouns. Remember that all proper nouns need capital letters.

Abstract Nouns	Proper Nouns
month	September
holiday	Presidents' Day
event	U.S. Open
country	Canada

Activity A On your paper, write a proper noun to match each common noun.

1. day
2. country
3. holiday
4. song

5. city
6. event
7. movie
8. language

9. sports team
10. book

The name of a person is a proper noun. A person's title is part of his or her name. **Capitalize** the first letter of each word in a person's title. To capitalize, use capital letters. When you use a short form, add a period.

EXAMPLE
President Lincoln
Queen Mary
Prince John
Senator Lyn Redmond

Dr. Maria Chang
Ms. Lisa Waters
Mrs. Leslie Conners
Mr. Steven Arnold

Activity B Write this list of words. Capitalize each proper noun. Some of the words are common nouns. Common nouns do not begin with capital letters.

1. mr. smith
2. detroit
3. statue of liberty
4. school
5. monday

6. city
7. senator
8. dr. adams
9. day
10. president washington

Canada

President

Day

Holiday

Detroit

Semicolons and commas must appear in compound sentences that use these conjunctions: *however, therefore, besides,* and *instead.*

A semicolon comes before the conjunction. A comma comes after the conjunction.

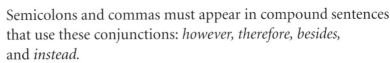

EXAMPLE   The ice melted into a puddle; however, I wiped it up.

Activity C Write each sentence on your paper. Add capital letters, commas, semicolons, and periods to make the sentences correct.

1. it rained therefore we left early

2. he wanted candy instead he ate fruit

3. ann brought her car besides we rode with her before

4. the sun set a new moon rose

5. dr adams mr allen and ms romone met senator lopez in the park

6. mr samuels beeped the horn however ms tompkins and mrs west had already left

7. mrs gomez greeted senator andrews during the labor day parade

8. mr edwards and ms keller watched prince charles on television

9. dr finch opened the door therefore mr lee handed him the package for mrs finch.

10. senator larsen explained the problem to mr boyd ms lake mr shobe and dr connors

Chapter 4   R E V I E W

Word Bank

abstract noun

capitalize

compound direct object

concrete noun

direct object

nominative pronoun

objective pronoun

pronoun

Part A On a sheet of paper, write the correct word or words from the Word Bank to complete each sentence.

1. A pronoun used as an object is an _____ .
2. A _____ receives action directly from the verb.
3. A _____ is two or more direct objects joined by a conjunction.
4. A word that names something that you cannot see or touch is an _____ .
5. A pronoun used as the subject of a sentence is a _____ .
6. A _____ is a word that takes the place of a noun.
7. To use capital letters is to _____ .
8. A _____ names something that you can see or touch.

Part B Write each sentence. Underline the subject once, underline the prepositional phrase twice, circle the verb, and draw an arrow to the direct object. If a sentence is compound, write *C.*

9. The students cleaned the vacant lot near the school.
10. They collected the trash on the ground.
11. Later, they planted some flowers in the dirt.
12. The students made a new park, and the neighbors thanked them with a party.

Part C Write each sentence. Replace each noun in bold with a pronoun. Write what part of the sentence the pronoun is: *subject, direct object,* or *object of the preposition.*

13. **Sarah** didn't like the **homework.**
14. Studying for the **test** was hard.
15. **Greg** studied with **Franklin** and **Ramon.**

Part D Write a proper noun for each common noun. Be sure to capitalize each proper noun.

16. month
17. state
18. landmark
19. person

Part E Write each sentence correctly.

20. ms cho met dr ray on monday march 17

21. i had an appointment however it was canceled

22. we grabbed our lunches ran out the door and got on the bus

Part F Read this paragraph. Then follow the directions for each item.

> Michelle plays the flute, and Lynda plays the guitar. The women often meet and practice music. Lynda and Michelle strum and toot songs and tunes. Sometimes a friend stops by, holds the music, and sings a tune with them. Michelle, Lynda, and the friend make a good sound and have fun during lazy summer nights.

23. Write the sentence that has a compound subject, compound verb, and compound direct object.

24. Write the compound sentence.

25. Find each of these words and tell its part of speech: *often, and, practice, with, lazy,* and *sometimes.*

26. Find three abstract nouns.

27. List the verbs along with any direct objects in the sentence that begins with an adverb.

Part G On your paper, write the letter that correctly completes the sentences or describes the word in bold.

28. Since Bo needed a tie, he bought one for _____ .

    A himself   **B** myself   **C** themselves   **D** ourselves

29. Please put _____ dishes near you on the counter.

    A that   **B** those   **C** this   **D** these

30. Helen took **that** suit to the cleaner.

    A pronoun   **B** noun   **C** adjective   **D** preposition

Test-Taking Tip Answer all questions you are sure of first; then go back and answer the others.

5

Practice with Parts of Speech

Do you remember how you learned to do something new? Maybe you just learned to drive. Maybe you learned how to use a new computer. Maybe you learned a new dance movement. At first the task seemed hard. It felt odd to be doing something you'd never done before. But it got easier each time you did it. The old saying "practice makes perfect" is true. It takes practice to master a new skill.

In this chapter, you will practice the parts of speech you have studied. You will study other parts of speech. You will also practice a four-step writing process.

Goals for Learning

◆ To identify parts of speech in different positions in a sentence

◆ To use owner nouns and pronouns correctly

◆ To use a variety of adverbs

◆ To recognize a sentence with an understood subject

◆ To identify and write interjections

◆ To apply the writing process

Some words in the English language can be more than one part of speech. The part of speech that a word is depends on the use of the word in a sentence.

You have learned about words that can be either prepositions or adverbs. There also are words that can be either nouns or verbs. Some words can be either nouns or adjectives. Other words can be either nouns, verbs, or adjectives.

EXAMPLE

Adverb	The teacher looked inside. (*Inside* tells where the teacher looked.)
Preposition	The teacher looked inside the room. (*Inside* introduces the adverb prepositional phrase *inside the room.*)
Noun	Sam starred in the show. (*Show* is the object of the preposition *in.*)
Verb	Show me the picture. (*Show* is the simple predicate. What do you do? You *show.*)
Noun	The test will be easy. (*Test* is the subject. What will be easy? The *test* will be easy.)
Adjective	Claude will be a test subject. (*Test* describes the noun *subject.* It tells what kind of subject.)
Noun	They saw a statue made of iron. (*Iron* is the object of the preposition *of.*)
Adjective	Jorge and Kendall walked to the iron statue. (*Iron* describes the noun *statue.* It tells which statue.)
Verb	Teresa and Rick iron the wrinkled clothes. (*Iron* is the simple predicate. What do Teresa and Rick do? They *iron.*)

Activity A On your paper, write the part of speech for each word in bold.

1. Ben and Karen take a long **drive.**
2. Karen will **drive** during the trip.
3. Karen will **park** the car near the **park** entrance.
4. They **walk** in the **park.**
5. During the **walk,** they pass by a **park** bench.

Some forms of verbs can be used as adjectives.

EXAMPLE	Verb	The water spilled. (*Spilled* is the simple predicate. What happened to the water? It *spilled*.)
	Adjective	The spilled water ruined the drawing. (*Spilled* describes the noun *water*. It tells which water.)

Ben and Karen walk in the park.

Activity B On your paper, write the part of speech for each word in bold.

1. Jasmeen writes a **check** for $100.
2. The **check** is for the man in the **checkered** shirt.
3. The man will **check** his **watch** and **watch** for Jasmeen.
4. Jasmeen phoned the man and **checked** in with him.
5. Dennis **scaled** a fish and weighed it on a **scale.**

Owner noun

A noun that owns something in a sentence

Apostrophe (')

A punctuation mark in an owner's name

Some nouns show ownership. A noun that shows ownership in a sentence is an **owner noun.** An owner noun may be a proper noun or a common noun.

Use an **apostrophe** plus *-s ('s)* to form an owner noun that tells about only one owner.

> **EXAMPLE** Roberta's car runs smoothly.
> (Whom does the car belong to? The car belongs to Roberta. *Roberta* is a proper noun.)
>
> The dog's toy rolled behind the tree.
> (Whom does the toy belong to? The toy belongs to the dog. *Dog* is a common noun.)
>
> The sink's drain leaks.
> (What does the drain belong to? The drain belongs to the sink. *Sink* is a common noun.)

An owner noun may show ownership of a common noun or an abstract noun.

> **EXAMPLE** We watched the singer's performance.
> (Whose performance did we watch? We watched the singer's performance. *Performance* is a common noun.)
>
> We discussed Kim's ideas.
> (Whose ideas did we discuss? We discussed Kim's ideas. *Ideas* is an abstract noun.)

M

a

x

1.

2.

Max's cat

sleeps

in the sun.

Activity A On your paper, write the second sentence in each pair of sentences with an owner noun.

Example   Maria has a sister.
          Maria's sister took her to the game.

1. Max has a cat.
_____ cat sleeps in the sun.

2. Tomas has a car.
_____ car made a wrong turn.

3. Jamal has a cold.
_____ cold kept him home from work.

4. Megan had a dream.
_____ dream was scary.

5. Kate has a brother.
_____ brother bought a new car.

Activity B Use the information in the box to complete each numbered item below with an owner noun. Write each completed item on your paper.

> The boy has a sleeping bag.
> The child has a book.
> The cat has a rubber mouse.
> The neighbor has a rake.
> The teenager has some tapes.
> The television has a cord.

When I came home, I tripped on

Example   the neighbor's rake,

1. the _____ rubber mouse,

2. the _____ book,

3. the _____ cord,

4. the _____ tapes, and

5. the _____ sleeping bag.

Max's cat sleeps in the sun.

You have learned that pronouns can take the place of nouns in a sentence. Pronouns that show ownership in a sentence are **owner pronouns.** Owner pronouns do not use apostrophes.

Owner pronoun

A pronoun that owns something in a sentence

Owner object

A noun following an owner pronoun or owner noun

Owner Pronouns	
One Owner	**Two or More Owners**
my	our
your	your
his	their
her	
its	

The noun following the owner pronoun or owner noun is the **owner object.**

Writing Tip

Another way to show possesion is to use a prepositional phrase with the preposition *of.*

Example: the car's engine—the engine of the car.

EXAMPLE

Stephan placed his glass on the counter.
(The owner pronoun *his* takes the place of the proper noun *Stephan. His* shows that the glass belongs to Stephan. *Glass* is the owner object.)

The truck lost its mirror.
(The owner pronoun *its* takes the place of the common noun *truck. Its* shows that the mirror belongs to the truck. *Mirror* is the owner object.)

The visitors left their papers on the table.
(The owner pronoun *their* takes the place of the common noun *visitors. Their* shows that the papers belong to the visitors. *Papers* is the owner object.)

Activity A Read each sentence. Find all the owner pronouns, and write them on your paper. Next to each owner pronoun, write the owner object.

Example Her cousin went around the block on my new scooter.

Her—cousin

my—scooter

1. Martin and I saw his sister at the movie.

2. Her dog and our cat play in their yard.

3. Your bus, with its orange sign, stops at her house.

4. His brother gestures with his hands to talk to their neighbor.

5. My sweater, your glove, and her scarf are here.

6. This is her book about Braille.

7. The woman learned to read Braille from her cousin.

8. Kamilla had polished her old car carefully.

9. Its left wheel had a flat tire during their last ride.

10. Their car showed its age.

Activity B Write each sentence on your paper. Fill in the blank with an owner pronoun. Look at the list of owner pronouns on page 96 for help.

Example We visited Nate at the ranch and rode <u>his</u> horse.

1. Lin and I picked berries from _____ garden.

2. We made a fruit salad, and _____ bright colors tempted everyone.

3. Mom shared _____ cooking secrets with us.

4. Dad gave _____ opinion to the cooks.

5. Coleta's brothers washed _____ hands and came to the table.

You have learned that an owner noun can show ownership by one owner. Owner nouns can also show ownership by more than one owner.

Use -s apostrophe (s') to form most owner nouns that show ownership by more than one owner.

EXAMPLE

One owner	The worker painted Mr. Jackson's house.
	(Mr. Jackson alone has a house.)
More than one owner	The worker painted the girls' cabinet.
	(Two or more girls share the cabinet.)

Owner pronouns can also show ownership by more than one owner.

EXAMPLE

| **More than one owner** | The pirates buried their treasure. |
| | (The owner pronoun *their* shows that the treasure belongs to more than one pirate.) |

Activity A Write each owner's name on your paper.

Example The performers have dances.
performers' dances

1. The kids have toys. _____ toys

2. The parks have paths. _____ paths

3. The horses have saddles. _____ saddles

4. The kittens have milk. _____ milk

5. The trucks have tires. _____ tires

Two people may own something together. For example, Kat and Jen may share a bedroom. To show this, add an apostrophe and -s to the last word in the word group: *Kat and Jen's room.*

Be careful when using a pronoun to take the place of a noun that names a group, such as *team, crowd, army,* and *committee.* Use the pronoun *it* to take the place of a noun that names a group.

 EXAMPLE **Group noun**   The stack of bricks fell.
              Pronoun   It fell.
                                (Although many bricks fell, only
                                one stack fell.)

Use the owner pronoun *its* to take the place of a group noun that shows ownership.

 EXAMPLE **Group noun**   The band's singer wrote the song.
              Pronoun   Its singer wrote the song.
                                (Although there are many
                                musicians in the band, there is
                                only one band.)

Activity B Write these sentences on your paper. Replace the words in bold with pronouns.

   1. The group left early.

   2. The cheerleaders' captain began a new cheer.

   3. The team scored.

   4. A player stole the ball from his opponent.

   5. The crowd yelled.

Activity C Write these sentences on your paper. Replace the words in bold with owner pronouns.

   1. The group's cheer made the rafters ring.

   2. The school's score rose after the cheer.

   3. The team's spirit rose, too.

   4. The crowd's yells grew.

   5. The band's music filled the gym.

Understood subject

A subject that cannot be seen in a sentence

Understood you

You as a subject that cannot be seen in a sentence

Every sentence has a subject. Prepositional phrases may make the subject hard to find. Just remember that the object of a preposition is *never* the subject of a sentence.

EXAMPLE   A lot of people waited.

	I I I I I
Parts of speech	*adj. noun prep. noun* *verb*
Sentence parts	subject with prepositional phrase I predicate
Sentence pattern	subject + verb

Some sentences have **understood subjects.** For example, a sentence spoken to *you* means that *you* are being asked to do something. It is an **understood *you*.** The subject of the sentence is understood to be *you*.

EXAMPLE   Pick up that trash.

	I I I I
Parts of speech	*verb adv. adj. noun*
Sentence pattern	(subject) + verb + direct object (*You* is the understood subject.)

The subject can be hard to find when the predicate comes before the subject of a sentence. These kinds of sentences often begin with the adverb *here* or *there*. To find the subject in these sentences, try turning the sentence around.

EXAMPLE   There goes the teacher.

	I I I I
Parts of speech	*adv. verb adj. noun*
	(To find the subject, turn the sentence around.)
	The teacher goes there.
	(Who goes? The *teacher* goes.)
Sentence pattern	subject + verb

Activity A On your paper, write the subject, verb, and direct object (if there is one) for each sentence. If the subject is understood, write *you*.

1. Akili earned a lot of money.
2. Come to my house.
3. Take me to work on Tuesday.
4. A lot of money sat on the table.
5. Catch that amazing show.
6. Watch my bag.
7. Many people want a lot of money.
8. Sit quietly and listen.
9. Raise your hand.
10. Turn left at Maple Lane.
11. A lot of trees stand by the road.
12. Look at that paper's ad.
13. Call your parents.
14. A lot of people like Tyler.
15. Read the next chapter by Friday.

Activity B On your paper, write each sentence so that the subject comes first. Underline the simple subject.

1. Here comes Alice with her friends.
2. Away fly the birds.
3. Here comes the train from New York.
4. There goes the group of children.
5. There lies the problem.

Do not be fooled by *here* or *there* at the beginning of these kinds of sentences. As adverbs, they tell *where*. The fastest way to find the subject of a sentence is to ask *who* or *what* is doing the action.

You have learned that adverbs describe verbs. Adverbs can also describe adjectives and other adverbs.

> **EXAMPLE**
>
> The very large package arrived too late.
>
> **Parts of speech** adj. adv. adj. noun verb adv. adv.
>
> **Sentence parts** subject | predicate
>
> (*Very* describes the adjective *large*. *Very* is an adverb. *Too* describes the adverb *late*. *Too* is an adverb.)

Try to avoid using *too* and *very* when another adverb will make your sentence more interesting. Here are some adverbs you can use in place of *too* and *very*.

almost	rather	terribly
awfully	really	totally
extremely	so	truly
quite	somewhat	unusually

Activity A On your paper, write the adverb in bold in each sentence. Then write the word it describes and its part of speech.

Example The taxi left the station **very** early.

very—early, adverb

1. The driver spent **too** many hours on the road.

2. The route covered **extremely** sharp curves.

3. Snow comes **quite** often in the mountains.

4. The bus arrived in an **unusually** bad storm.

5. Alan waited a **really** long time for the bus.

Activity B Choose a word other than *too* or *very* to fill in these blanks. Write the words on your paper.

1. Our _____ snowy winter made a good sports season.
2. Ice and snow made the ski trails _____ slick.
3. Skaters glide _____ fast across the frozen lake.
4. People need to be _____ careful in the winter.
5. The _____ cold winter damaged trees and shrubs.
6. Icy ruts made the roads _____ dangerous.
7. Some people stayed inside during the _____ long winter.
8. Fields of snow glared in the _____ bright sun.
9. _____ strong winds flattened the old barn.
10. _____ long chunks of ice hung from the roof.

Skiers enjoy the snowy weather.

Interjection

A word that shows feelings

An **interjection** is a word that expresses feeling. An interjection often comes first in a sentence.

> **EXAMPLE** Oh, the ice melted.
> Hey! It's all over the carpet.
> (*Oh* and *hey* are both interjections.)

Writing Tip

Interjections are a good way to make your writing more interesting. Use interjections only in informal writing.

Here are some words that are used as interjections:

hurray	good-bye	zap
hush	gee whiz	whoosh
hello	ah	boy
ouch	gosh	pow
wow	well	hey
oh	yuck	ha
yikes	aha	no

Activity A Write each sentence on your paper. Fill in the blank with an interjection from the list above.

1. _____! Antonio won a large amount of money.

2. _____! The new worker on the night shift works hard.

3. _____! That small airplane landed safely in the dense fog.

4. _____! The thick ropes snapped during the daring rescue at sea.

5. _____! A black motorcycle roared through the quiet streets.

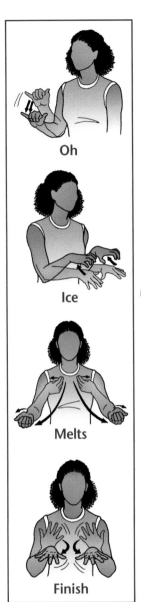

Oh

Ice

Melts

Finish

Oh, the ice melted.

Activity B Write each sentence on your paper. Fill in the blank with an interjection of your choice.

1. _____! I forgot to buy bread.
2. _____! Maybe I can stop at that store.
3. _____! Look at the huge bread selection
4. _____! I don't think I can make a decision.
5. _____! This bread is expensive.

Do not confuse interjections with adverbs that begin a sentence. Remember, adverbs tell about verbs, adjectives, or other adverbs. Interjections express feelings. They do not tell about any other word in the sentence.

EXAMPLE

Adverb	Honestly, Julie spoke to her mother. (*Honestly* is an adverb that tells about the verb *spoke*. How did Julie speak? She spoke *honestly*.)
Interjection	Honestly! I did not break the window. (*Honestly* is an interjection that expresses the subject's feelings. *Honestly* does not tell about any other word in the sentence.)

Activity C Write whether the word in bold is an adverb or an interjection.

1. **Hush,** the baby is sleeping.
2. **Ugh!** I really disliked that movie.
3. **Perhaps** you did not understand it.
4. **Maybe,** Ravi left early.
5. **Oh,** I miss him.

Writing process

The use of four steps: prewrite, write, rewrite, and edit

Prewrite

Talking, thinking, or reading about a topic before writing

Write

Putting ideas on paper

Rewrite

Writing again until the meaning is clear

Edit

Checking written work for mistakes

Writing is a way to express your feelings and ideas. Writing well takes practice. The **writing process** can help you develop good ideas. It can help you focus your thoughts and present them clearly to your readers.

The writing process has four steps: **prewrite, write, rewrite,** and **edit.**

1. **Prewrite.** The first thing you do before writing is decide what you want to write about. Gather your thoughts. Write them down on paper or note cards. Then arrange your notes so that they make sense.

2. **Write.** Write a first draft, or copy. Write your ideas as clearly as you can, but don't worry about mistakes. You can correct mistakes later.

3. **Rewrite.** You want your writing to express your meaning. Go back and read what you wrote. Can it be improved? Rewrite any sentences that are unclear.

4. **Edit.** Now read your work and look for mistakes in spelling, punctuation, or sentence structure. Be sure to correct all the mistakes you find.

Activity A Read each group of sentences. Then choose one group. Add adverbs, adjectives, compounds, and prepositional phrases to the sentences to write a short story. Use the steps of the writing process.

1. A Andres and Regina sit.

   B Andres and Regina play chess.

   C People watch.

   D Regina wins the prize.

   E Regina and Andres leave.

2. A Rachel bakes rolls.

 B Rachel bakes bread.

 C Rachel slices bread.

 D Rachel serves bread.

 E Rachel sells baked goods.

3. A Fish swim.

 B Bruce wades.

 C Bruce casts.

 D Bruce reels.

 E Bruce catches fish.

4. A Eddie chases.

 B Nick runs.

 C Nick hides.

 D Eddie searches.

 E Nick waits.

5. A Kyle digs.

 B Kyle plants.

 C Sun shines.

 D Rain falls.

 E Tree grows.

You have learned to form owner nouns with apostrophes. Use apostrophe and -*s* to show one owner. Use -*s* and an apostrophe to show more than one owner.

Activity A Write each sentence correctly on your paper. Remember that every sentence begins with a capital letter and ends with a punctuation mark.

1. the mans suit hangs in the closet
2. many trucks tires littered the road
3. frans brother owns a theater
4. four ships sails snapped in the wind
5. a birds nest fell from the branch

An exclamation point or a comma follows interjections that begin a sentence.

An exclamation point is a punctuation mark used when you want to show strong feeling. Use an exclamation point after an interjection that shows strong feelings.

> **EXAMPLE**   Yikes! I almost fell off the chair.
> Aha! We caught the dog.

Use a comma after an interjection that shows mild feelings.

> **EXAMPLE**   Gee, that book ended sadly.
> Well, we finished our project on time.

Activity B Decide what feeling you want the interjection to show. Then write each sentence correctly.

 1. well i found my house

 2. ouch you stepped on my foot

 3. quick turn on the lights

 4. ah i found my shoe

 5. oh i fell across the coffee table

 6. boom thunder rattled the house

 7. crack lightning hit the roof

 8. zzzt lightning zapped the stereo the TV and the CD player

 9. oh the lightning could have started a fire

10. wow Krista will never forget that terrible night

Activity C Match the words with their meanings. Write the number and its correct letter on your paper.

Words	Meanings
1. apostrophe	**A** shows feelings
2. interjection	**B** !
3. owner pronouns	**C** tells word order
4. sentence pattern	**D** mark that shows ownership
5. exclamation point	**E** my, his, her, its, your, their

Using What You've Learned

Write a paragraph about something that frightened or surprised you or someone else. Use an interjection in at least three sentences.

Chapter 5   R E V I E W

Word Bank

apostrophe

edit

interjection

owner noun

owner object

owner pronoun

prewrite

rewrite

understood subject

understood *you*

write

writing process

Part A   Read each sentence below. Fill in each blank with a vocabulary word that correctly completes each sentence.

1. An _____ is a noun that shows ownership in a sentence.

2. The process that helps you use the four writing steps to present your ideas in writing is called the _____.

3. Use an _____ plus -*s* to form an owner noun.

4. You _____ when you put your ideas on paper.

5. A pronoun used to show ownership in a sentence is called an _____.

6. To write again until the meaning is clear is to _____.

7. An _____ is a noun following an owner pronoun or owner noun.

8. To talk, think, or read about a topic before writing is to _____.

9. A subject that cannot be seen in a sentence is called an _____.

10. You _____ when you check written work for mistakes.

11. The _____ is *you* as a subject that cannot be seen in a sentence.

12. You use an _____ when you want to show feelings.

Part B   Read this paragraph. Answer the questions on your paper.

> After work, Carlo looks at the used car for sale. The car's doors have dents. The door's dents are not bad though. Carlo's friend bought a car. His car has a dent, too. Gee, Carlo still wants this car for work and school.

13. Write the sentence that has an interjection.

14. Write the owner pronoun.

15. Write all the owner nouns with their owner objects. Circle the owner nouns.

Part C Write these sentences correctly.

16. wow look at that beautiful sunset

17. several spiders webs filled the old barn

18. the red cars door fell off during the race

Part D Write the correct part of speech for each word in bold.

19. Adrienne and Julie **talk** to each other by e-mail.
   A verb   **B** noun   **C** adjective   **D** adverb

20. One night they had a long **talk** about TV shows.
   A adverb   **B** verb   **C** adjective   **D** noun

21. They discussed a **talk** show about rap music.
   A adverb   **B** adjective   **C** verb   **D** preposition

Part E Write the understood subject, the verb, and the direct object for each sentence.

22. See the new models in the showroom.

23. Send both boxes to me.

24. Wow! Feel the beat of the music.

Part F Add adverbs, adjectives, compounds, and prepositional phrases to these sentences. Use the writing process to write a short story.

25. Dog walks.

26. Cat runs.

27. Dog chases.

28. Cat turns.

29. Cat hides.

30. Dog barks.

Test-Taking Tip Take time to organize your thoughts before writing answers to short-answer questions.

6

More Sentence Patterns

Patterns, whether in nature or in writing, can lead you to look at something more closely. Patterns attract the eye and grab your attention. They demonstrate a sense of order. Look at the intricate patterns in this garden photograph. Every item in the garden has its place. Nothing is random. Color, contrast, and shape make the garden appealing.

Likewise, the parts of a sentence are not random; each part of a sentence has its proper place. Sentences follow certain patterns just like the patterns in the garden. In Chapter 6, you will learn about sentence patterns. You can make your writing more appealing and give it color, contrast, and shape by using what you learn about sentence patterns.

Goals for Learning

◆ To identify indirect objects and object complements

◆ To recognize sentences with indirect objects and object complements

◆ To identify and write appositives

◆ To identify and write sentences that use different sentence patterns

◆ To use correct punctuation with appositives

Indirect object

A noun or pronoun that takes action from the verb indirectly

Notice that the indirect object usually comes between the verb and the direct object.

Example
The teacher reads **us** a story.

Sentences with direct objects may also have **indirect objects.** An indirect object is a noun or pronoun that takes action from the verb indirectly. An indirect object answers the question *to whom, to what, for whom,* or *for what* about the verb.

EXAMPLE   The teacher reads a story.

Parts of speech   adj.   noun   verb   adj.   noun
Sentence pattern   subject + verb + direct object

The same sentence can have an indirect object.

                     The teacher reads us a story.

Parts of speech   adj.   noun   verb   pron.   adj.   noun
Sentence pattern   subject + verb + indirect object +
                     direct object

(The teacher reads the story to whom? The teacher reads the story *to us. Us* is a pronoun used as an indirect object. *Story* is the direct object.)

If you are not sure which word in the sentence is the indirect object, try this: Put *to* or *for* in front of the noun or pronoun. If the sentence still makes sense, the noun is the indirect object.

EXAMPLE   The teacher gave Jack extra credit.
       Try   The teacher gave extra credit to Jack.

                  Ellie saved Anna the last bottle of water.
       Try   Ellie saved the last bottle of water for Anna.

(The sentences make sense both ways. In the first pair of sentences, *Jack* is the indirect object of the verb *gave. Credit* is the direct object. In the second pair of sentences, *Anna* is the indirect object of the verb *saved. Bottle* is the direct object.)

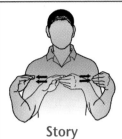

Story

Teacher

Read

We

Finish

Activity A On your paper, write the indirect object in each of these sentences. Remember that an indirect object answers the question *to whom, to what, for whom,* or *for what* about the verb.

1. Alejandro asked Ms. Wilson some questions about the lesson.
2. She gave Alejandro the answers.
3. Homework provides students extra practice.
4. The teacher hands Alejandro a report card.
5. The new term offers Alejandro new things to learn.

Activity B Write the word in bold on your paper. Then write whether it is a *direct object* or an *indirect object.*

Example   Jenny bought **Fran** lunch at the restaurant.
             Fran—indirect object

1. Mr. Tan paid **Jenny** twenty dollars for mowing his lawn.
2. The clerk handed Jenny the **bill** for lunch.
3. She paid the **clerk** six dollars.
4. The clerk gave her a little **change.**
5. Jenny lent Fran **money.**
6. Fran bought **them** drinks.
7. She gave **Jenny** a cold bottle of juice.
8. Jenny's friend told **her** a silly joke.
9. Jenny gave her friend a wide **smile.**
10. Fran's brother Lou offered the girls a **ride** home.

The teacher read us a story.

Sentences with indirect objects may have compound parts and prepositional phrases that add information to the sentence. By identifying the basic parts of the sentence, you can identify the indirect object.

> **EXAMPLE** The principal and the student with the blue backpack on her shoulders asked the basketball coach a question at the same time.
>
> **Compound subject**   principal, student
> **Verb**   asked
> **Indirect object**   coach
> **Direct object**   question

Although the example sentence appears long and complicated, it follows the basic sentence pattern of *subject + verb + indirect object + direct object.* Remove the adjectives and prepositional phrases, and you can easily recognize the sentence pattern.

> **EXAMPLE** The principal and student asked the coach a question.
>
> **Sentence pattern**   subject + verb + indirect obj. + direct obj.

Activity A Write the indirect object in these sentences on your paper. (Hint: To find the indirect object, find the verb. Ask *to whom, to what, for whom,* or *for what* about the verb.)

1. The boy and girl in the back seat of the car told their mom riddles during the long ride home.

2. The frisky little puppy with the red collar brought the young boy on the porch the ball.

3. The radio announcer offered listeners of his early morning program a free holiday turkey.

4. Passengers on the flight from Boston to Denver handed the flight attendant at the boarding gate their tickets.

5. The football coach on the bus taught the team plays before the game.

Activity B Write these sentences on your paper. Label the
simple subject *S*, the verb *V*, the direct object *DO*, and the
indirect object *IO*. Some sentences may have compound parts.

          S   V   IO   DO

Example   Jack drew Emily a picture on a large piece of
           white paper.

1. The other students in the room asked Jack a question
   about his picture.

2. Jack taught the group his art style and showed Emily
   his picture.

3. Some of the students gave Jack a pat on the back for
   his efforts.

4. Jack gave shy Emily his drawing of her.

5. She sent him her thanks with a smile.

6. Gus and Rose Thompson bought themselves a farm.

7. The Thompson family's hard work on the farm brought
   them a good life.

8. The herd of cows gave the family good, rich milk.

9. Gus fed the chickens lots of mash and seed.

10. The hens gave the family dozens of eggs.

11. The oldest daughter fixed the younger children large
    breakfasts of eggs, bacon, and milk.

12. Rose taught her oldest daughter the farm chores.

13. Rose's work in the city brought the farm more money
    for repairs.

14. Their son built the animals a new barn with large stalls
    for the horses.

15. Farm life offered Gus, Rose, and their children joy
    and profit.

Object complement

A word or words that follow the direct object and describe or rename it

Adjective object complement

An adjective that describes the direct object

Noun object complement

A noun that renames the direct object

Sentences with direct objects may also have **object complements.** An object complement is an adjective, a noun, or a pronoun that describes or renames the direct object. An object complement follows the direct object. Like other sentence parts, an object complement may be compound.

An **adjective object complement** follows the direct object and describes it.

EXAMPLE   The girl painted the flower red.

Sentence parts   *subj.*   *v.*   *d. obj.   adj. compl.*

(The adjective *red* describes the direct object *flower.*)

The hikers found the children uninjured and safe.

Sentence parts   *subj.*   *v.*   *d. obj.   adj. compl.*

(The adjectives *uninjured* and *safe* describe the direct object *children.*)

A **noun object complement** is a noun or pronoun that follows the direct object and renames it.

EXAMPLE   My cousin named the fish Goldie.

Sentence parts   *subj.*   *v.*   *d. obj.   noun compl.*

(The proper noun *Goldie* renames the direct object *fish.*)

They consider that player a talented one.

Sentence parts   *subj.*   *v.*   *d. obj.   noun compl.*

(The pronoun *one* renames the direct object *player.*)

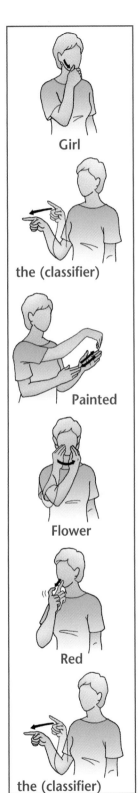

Girl

the (classifier)

Painted

Flower

Red

the (classifier)

The girl painted the flower red.

Activity A Write the adjectives that are object complements in these sentences on your paper.

1. Jane likes her soup hot.
2. Most people prefer crackers crisp.
3. Cinnamon makes cereal tasty.
4. Andreas likes his soup hot and his sandwiches cold.
5. He wants his salads fresh and his apples crunchy.
6. Stella painted her car blue and gold.
7. Max liked his car red and white.
8. Mitsu built her bike low and sleek.
9. Janet wanted her car beautiful and fast.
10. She got a car that was rusty and slow.

Activity B Write the nouns or pronouns that are object complements in these sentences on your paper.

1. The young man called his old uncle a true friend.
2. The voters in his state elected José senator.
3. Jane called her friends good sports.
4. That movie made the actor a famous person.
5. Many people find that movie an exciting one.

Activity C Fill in the blank with an object complement. Write each completed sentence on your paper.

1. Spice makes food _____ .
2. Phil likes his bread _____ .
3. The man called his friend _____ .
4. Rita named her puppy _____ .
5. Sun turned her skin _____ .

Sentences with object complements may have compound parts and prepositional phrases. By identifying the basic parts of the sentence, you can identify the object complement.

> **EXAMPLE** On their vacation, the boy and his parents named the rented house in the woods beside the lake Home Base.
>
> | **Compound subject** | boy, parents |
> | --- | --- |
> | **Verb** | named |
> | **Direct object** | house |
> | **Object complement** | Home Base |

Although the example sentence has compound parts, adjectives, and adjective phrases, it still follows the basic sentence pattern of *subject + verb + direct object + object complement.* Remove the adjectives and prepositional phrases, and you can easily recognize the sentence pattern.

> **EXAMPLE**
>
> The boy and his parents named the house Home Base.
> subject · · · · · · · · · · · · verb · · d. obj. · · noun complement

Activity A On your paper, write the object complement in each sentence. Write whether the complement is an *adjective,* a *noun,* or a *pronoun.*

1. In the moonlight over the water, a pilot finds the night a lonely one.

2. At sunset on the pier, a crowd calls the band terrific.

3. By the gate in the park, the girls found a picnic table empty.

4. Down the rutted road through the woods, the driver in the old truck found the road a bumpy mess.

5. Lots of training made the dog a good hunter.

Activity B On your paper, make a chart like the one shown. In the chart write the words that form the basic sentence pattern in these sentences.

Example   Hours of practice in the pool made the swimmer fast and strong.

subject + verb + direct object + object complement			
Hours	made	swimmer	fast, strong

1. The new houses and the park made that street a pretty part of town.
2. The quick mechanic kept his tools handy.
3. Some flowering plants need their soil moist.
4. Herds of cattle and horses made the rancher a rich woman.
5. The people in Westown elected Sam Saltz mayor for two years.

Activity C On your paper, write whether the word in bold is a *direct object,* an *indirect object,* an *object of a preposition,* or an *object complement.*

1. Miguel told **him** the final score of the swim meet.
2. Steven quickly passed the news to the **class.**
3. The wonderful news gave the whole class a **thrill.**
4. The boys on the swim team told their **friends** the news.
5. The news made everyone at school and around town **happy.**

The swimmers race to be the fastest.

Appositive

A word or group of words that follows a noun and explains the noun or gives another name to the noun

An **appositive** explains a noun or gives another name to a noun. An appositive may be a single word or a group of words. When an appositive is a group of words, commas usually set it off from the rest of the sentence.

> **EXAMPLE**
>
> My uncle Antonio works at a bank.
> (*Antonio* is an appositive that gives another name to the noun *uncle.*)
>
> Ms. Levo, the school principal, walked down the hall.
> (*The school principal* is an appositive that explains who Ms. Levo is. Commas set off the appositive from the rest of the sentence.)

An appositive follows a noun in a sentence. The noun may be the subject, the direct object, the indirect object, or the object of a preposition.

> **EXAMPLE**
>
> His sister Kara moved to Toronto.
> (The appositive *Kara* renames the subject *sister.*)
>
> Emiko got a present, a bicycle.
> (The appositive *a bicycle* explains the direct object *present.*)
>
> Maria sent my cousin Maya a new coat.
> (The appositive *Maya* renames the indirect object *cousin.*)
>
> The boys climbed into the back seat of the car, a convertible.
> (The appositive *a convertible* explains *car,* the object of the preposition *of.*)

An appositive may have a prepositional phrase.

> **EXAMPLE**
>
> The dress, a fancy one with lace, tore.
> (*A fancy one with lace* is the appositive. *With lace* is a prepositional phrase that is part of the appositive.)

Activity A On your paper, write each sentence. Circle the appositive. Underline the noun the appositive explains or renames. Some sentences may have more than one appositive.

1. The grassy yard, part of a large ranch, glistened in the early morning dew.

2. A barn, the largest building, sits behind the house.

3. Frank, a rancher, gives Joe, the ranch foreman, instructions.

4. A green tractor, one of five, sits near the barn.

5. George, a ranch worker, began to plow the field, a large area.

Activity B On your paper, write the appositive in each sentence. Then write whether it names the *subject,* the *direct object,* or the *object of preposition.*

1. The pirates, a group of thieves, counted their treasure.

2. Big Bart, the leader, buried the huge chest.

3. Bart sailed his boat, a fast ship, into the night.

4. Jenny dug up the chest, a rich prize.

5. Jenny yelled to Amy, her friend, to come and help her.

Activity C Add an appositive to each sentence to rename or explain the noun in bold. Write the sentences on your paper. Use commas where needed to set off appositives.

Example Anna received an invitation to a **party.**
Anna received an invitation to a party, a surprise birthday celebration for Melissa.

1. **Anna** went to a wonderful party in the city.

2. She met a tall **boy.**

3. They listened to the music of a great **band.**

4. The **music** was lively and fun.

5. Two dancers taught a new line **dance.**

Writing is hard but fun. You never know where your thoughts might lead you. You can start with a list of words and end with a story. Another student can begin with the same list of words but write a very different story.

Activity A Using the following list of subjects and direct objects, write ten clear sentences on your paper using action verbs. You may use any subject with any direct object.

Subjects	
horse	hero
cat	pitcher
writer	friend
grandmother	sister
teacher	monster

Direct Objects	
money	grass
dinner	television
book	paper
tree	job
game	ball

The pitcher tosses the ball to the batter.

Activity B Using the sentences you wrote in Activity A, add adjectives, adverbs, and prepositional phrases to improve your sentences. Choose from this box, or write your own.

Adjectives	
huge	kind
bleak	friendly
fast	ugly
old	young
brave	beautiful
Adverbs	
slowly	quietly
quickly	wildly
often	poorly
well	gladly
loudly	gently
Prepositional Phrases	
over the hill	on the chair
to the batter	at the desk
under the table	behind a tree
for a month	in the house
from the fire	around the bend

Activity C Write a story using the list of nouns and appositives below. Before you begin, think about what you want to write. Be sure to use the four-step writing process.

Nouns	Appositives
Buddy	cat
kitten	a lively animal
Grace	a lonely child

Use commas with appositives that are more than one word long. One-word appositives do not usually need commas, but you can use them.

Communication Connection

People use e-mail to send each other e-cards. E-cards have become a popular way to send birthday and holiday greetings. E-cards can even include music for the occasion. Have you ever received an e-card?

EXAMPLE   Ian, my cousin from Alberta, sent me an e-card.
(The long appositive *my cousin from Alberta* needs commas to set it off.)

Correct   My cousin Ian sent me an e-card.

Correct   My cousin, Ian, sent me an e-card.
(The one-word appositive *Ian* does not need commas to set it off, but you can use them.)

Activity A Write these sentences on your paper. Add any needed commas. Remember that long appositives need commas.

1. Tony's bike a rocket with wheels roared.

2. Two rabbits scared animals stared into the headlights.

3. They jumped into the ditch a safer place.

4. The moon a beaming light shone on the bikers' helmets.

5. Ann and her best friend Tony rode home together.

Use commas with items in a series. A series is a list of three or more words or phrases connected by a conjunction, such as *and*, *but*, or *or*. Do not put a comma after the last item in a series.

EXAMPLE   Dave, Anita, and Salma enjoyed their trip to Calgary.
(*Dave, Anita,* and *Salma* are nouns in a series.)

They rode down the highway, over a mountain, and through a city on their journey.
(*Down the highway, over a mountain,* and *through a city* are prepositional phrases in a series.)

Activity B Write these sentences correctly on your paper. Use commas, periods, exclamation points, and capital letters. You might wish to review what you have learned about writing sentences in previous lessons.

1. wow the batter the teams star hitter knocked the ball over the fence out of the park and down the street

2. down the alley a chill raw winter wind blew

3. bill and senator jacobs visited friends in new york city

4. ms adams mr smith and dr young sat near the stage at the play

5. bills mother a nice woman had us over for dinner

Activity C Match the items with their descriptions. Write the number and its correct letter on your paper.

Items
1. indirect object
2. noun object complement
3. adjective object complement
4. appositive
5. comma

Descriptions
A noun or pronoun that renames the direct object
B needed with a long appositive
C takes action from the verb indirectly
D adjective that describes the direct object
E gives a noun a new name

Chapter 6   R E V I E W

Word Bank

adjective object
complement

appositive

indirect object

noun object
complement

object
complement

Part A   Use the words from the Word Bank to complete sentences 1–5.

1. A word or group of words that follows a noun and explains the noun or gives another name to the noun is an _____ .

2. An _____ is a word or words that follow the direct object and describe or rename it.

3. A noun that renames the direct object is a _____ .

4. A noun or pronoun that takes action from the verb indirectly is an _____ .

5. An _____ is an adjective that describes the direct object.

Part B   Write the words in bold in these sentences. Next to each word write its sentence part.

Example   The club sent my **brother** a **letter**.
           brother—indirect object, letter—direct object

6. The farmer fed the **pigs** a bushel of **apples**.

7. Some **anglers** like the sky **cloudy**.

8. The pitcher **threw** the catcher a **look**.

9. Jeffrey **mailed Elisha** a package of CDs.

10. Adam likes the kitchen **window open**.

11. **Andrea** gave the **chickens** some water.

12. Years on the **job** at the factory made Dennis a skillful **employee**.

13. The TV program left **Patty sad**.

Part C   Write each sentence correctly on your paper. Underline each appositive, and circle the word it describes.

14. the cowboy a thin dude played a tune at the ranch

15. the sky a mass of black clouds closed over the ranch

16. the cook a friendly person greets ranch guests at the door

17. the guests nature lovers hoped for clear weather

Part D Use the sentence in parentheses to add an appositive to each sentence. Write the revised sentences on your paper.

Example   Emilio scored six goals. (Emilio is a fine athlete.)
Emilio, a fine athlete, scored six goals.

18. Jenny's computer solved the problem easily. (The computer is a powerful machine.)

19. Tony serves the best lobster in town. (Tony is a great cook.)

20. Jerome Cullen steered his ship. (Jerome Cullen is a captain.)

21. Concetta burned a fast ball to the catcher. (Concetta is the best pitcher in the league.)

22. Alejandro e-mailed Holly. (Holly is his best friend.)

Part E Read each sentence. Write the letter of the correct sentence pattern.

23. The students find this computer game easy.

A subject + verb
B subject + verb + direct object
C subject + verb + indirect object + direct object
D subject + verb + direct object + object complement

24. Isaiah sold his computer.

A subject + verb
B subject + verb + direct object
C subject + verb + indirect object + direct object
D subject + verb + direct object + object complement

25. That computer program gives me problems.

A subject + verb
B subject + verb + direct object
C subject + verb + indirect object + direct object
D subject + verb + direct object + object complement

Test-Taking Tip When you take a test, be sure to read each question carefully before answering.

Sentences with Linking Verbs

How might you describe this scene? First, you could say that the girl's reflection is in the window. A reflection is a mirror image. It looks almost the same as the real object, but it is slightly different. The girl's hand seems to connect her to her image. In a similar way, certain words in a sentence reflect on the subject. Predicate nouns rename the subject in different words. Like the girl's hand, linking verbs connect the subject with the predicate noun that renames, or reflects, it.

The girl's reflection shows how she looks, but it reverses her image. You can see her face in a new way. Some sentences have adjectives in the predicate that describe the subject. These predicate adjectives reflect the subject, but they show it in a new light.

In this chapter, you will study more about how words give detailed information and help you reflect, or think back, on what comes before them.

Goals for Learning

◆ To identify linking verbs and sentence patterns that use them

◆ To identify and use subject complements in sentences

◆ To distinguish between adjectives and adverbs

◆ To use pronouns in subject complement sentences

◆ To use comparative and superlative adjectives correctly

Subject complement

One or more words in the predicate that describe the subject

Noun subject complement

A noun or pronoun in the predicate that renames the subject, as well as any words that describe the noun or pronoun

Linking verb

A verb that connects the subject to a word in the predicate

A **subject complement** describes the subject of a sentence. A **noun subject complement** is a noun or pronoun in the predicate that gives a new name to the subject, along with any words that describe the noun or pronoun. Remember that a sentence has two parts: the subject and the predicate. A noun (or pronoun) in the predicate may rename the subject. A **linking verb** links the predicate with the subject.

 EXAMPLE   This soup is a favorite snack.
Sentence parts   subject | predicate
Sentence pattern   subject + linking verb +
                       noun subject complement
(The linking verb *is* in this sentence links the subject *soup* with a noun in the predicate *snack. A favorite snack* is the noun subject complement.)

Activity A On your paper, write the subject in each sentence. Then write the noun in the predicate that is linked to the subject by the linking verb. The linking verb is in bold.

Example   That police officer **is** my neighbor.
                officer—neighbor

1. Tennis **is** your favorite game.

2. Football **is** my best sport.

3. Haley **is** a speedy worker.

4. Jacob and Isaac **are** fast runners.

5. Sophia and David **were** neighbors.

A noun subject complement has another name: predicate nominative. The word *nominative* refers to the subject of a sentence.

Activity B On your paper, write the noun subject complement in each sentence. The linking verb in each sentence is in bold.

Example   Samuel **is** a busy director.
                    a busy director

1. Many of his movies **are** exciting adventures.
2. He **is** a popular movie director.
3. Most of his movies **are** box office hits.
4. My friends and I **are** loyal fans.
5. Emilio **is** the band's leader.
6. This band **is** a good one.
7. Melita, Jenny, and Christa **are** marchers.
8. The school band **is** a talented group.
9. The plot of this book **is** an exciting one.
10. The book's hero **was** a doctor.
11. Her friends **were** scientists.
12. Their enemy **was** fever.
13. Their job **was** a hard one.
14. A new medicine **was** their discovery.
15. Their victory **was** a breakthrough.

Activity C Complete each of these sentences with a noun subject complement. Write the sentences on your paper.

1. Their trip to Africa was _____ .
2. My aunt and uncle are _____ .
3. That story is _____ .
4. Good friends are _____ .
5. Lincoln and Grant were _____ .

There are three ways that a noun or a pronoun can give a new name to another noun in the sentence. Notice the different ways to rename the noun *salad* in each of the following examples.

> **EXAMPLE**
>
> | | |
> |---|---|
> | **Noun object complement** | I made the salad a big one. |
> | **Appositive** | The salad, a tropical fruit mix, chilled in the refrigerator. |
> | **Noun subject complement** | The fruit salad was a nice treat. |

Sometimes you can rename a noun in the subject in more than one place in a sentence.

> **EXAMPLE**
>
> The manager, a clever woman, is an amazing worker.
>
>   subject   appositive   noun subject complement
>
> (The subject noun *manager* is renamed twice: first, by the noun *woman* in the appositive *a clever woman;* and second, by the noun *worker* in the noun subject complement *an amazing worker.*)

Activity A On your paper, write each noun in bold. Next to each noun, write the noun object complement, appositive, or noun subject complement that renames it.

Example My **boss,** an organized man, straightened out his office.
boss—an organized man

1. **Takeo** and **Helen,** our new neighbors, are a busy couple.

2. The **coach,** a happy guy, is also our teacher and friend.

3. The country **woman,** a shy person, found the city a noisy place.

4. The **library,** a room full of books, was a quiet place.

5. Those two young **men,** clerks at the store, are helpful people.

You can write sentences with appositives and subject complements. Follow these steps:

1. Identify the parts of the sentence.
   Subject: girl
   Appositive: student
   Subject complement: writer

2. Write the sentence. Use the linking verb *is* or *was*.
   The girl, a student, is a writer.

3. Add adjectives to describe the nouns.
   The quiet girl, a bright student, is a good writer.

Activity B Use each group of words below to write a sentence with an appositive and a subject complement. Follow the steps described above.

1. cat, pet, friend
2. woman, singer, dancer
3. building, house, home
4. dog, puppy, animal
5. skater, athlete, winner
6. man, worker, carpenter
7. woman, neighbor, pilot
8. parrot, bird, pet
9. book, favorite, thriller
10. actor, star, performer

Activity C Write the groups of words in bold on your paper. Then write whether the group of words in bold is a *noun object complement*, an *appositive*, or a *noun subject complement*.

Example The baseball game was **an important one.**
an important one—noun subject complement

1. Michael, **the coach,** was very nervous.
2. The coach knew the game was **a big event.**
3. His players were **hard workers.**
4. His team, **the home team,** won the game.
5. The players were **the city champions.**

Lesson **3** Adjective Subject Complements

Adjective subject complement

One or more adjectives in the predicate that describe the subject

An adjective in the predicate of a sentence may describe the subject noun. The adjective is an **adjective subject complement.**

EXAMPLE

Parts of speech	This bread is expensive.

Parts of speech   This bread is expensive.
                        | | | |
                        adj. noun verb adj.

Sentence pattern   subject + linking verb +
                        adjective subject complement

(The linking verb *is* links the subject noun *bread* to the adjective in the predicate *expensive*. *Expensive* is the adjective subject complement.)

Some linking verbs are also action verbs. To check a verb's use in a sentence, replace it with a form of *be* or *seem*. If the sentence still makes sense, the verb is a linking verb.

An adjective subject complement always follows a linking verb. Remember that a linking verb connects the predicate with the subject.

Here is a list of linking verbs:

am	been	is	sound
appear	being	look	taste
are	feel	seem	was
be	grow	smell	were

Activity A On your paper, write the adjective subject complement in each sentence.

1. These two good friends are close.
2. Their clothes are old and worn.
3. Their pockets and stomachs are empty.
4. Their travels were exciting.
5. Their smiles are warm and friendly.

136   *Chapter 7   Sentences with Linking Verbs*

Activity B Write these sentences on your paper. Underline the linking verb in each sentence. Draw an arrow from the adjective subject complement to the subject in bold.

Example The **soup** at that restaurant <u>tastes</u> delicious.

1. Their fresh **vegetables** are terrific.
2. The **salads** look great.
3. The **bread** smells wonderful.
4. Each **customer** seems happy.
5. The **wait** seems long.

Activity C Complete each sentence with an adjective subject complement. Write the sentences on your paper.

1. The country seems _____ .
2. The farms appear _____ .
3. The breeze feels _____ .
4. The mountains look _____ .
5. The country food tastes _____ .
6. The city is _____ .
7. The crowded streets are _____ .
8. City people are _____ .
9. City lights are _____ .
10. City life is _____ .

In the city, people rush to and from work.

An adjective always describes a noun in a sentence. Most adjectives come right before the nouns they describe. An adjective may, however, follow the noun it describes or be separated from the noun by a linking verb.

Notice the placement of the adjectives that describe the noun *bear* in these sentences.

EXAMPLE

Adjectives before a noun	The hungry, brown bear growled.
Adjective object complement	Someone called the bear large.
Adjective subject complement	To me, the bear seemed huge.

More than one adjective may describe a noun. These adjectives may come before or after the noun.

EXAMPLE

I find the young pianist clever.
(The adjectives *young* and *clever* both describe the noun *pianist*. *Clever* is an adjective object complement.)

Activity A On your paper, write the adjectives that describe the nouns in bold in these sentences.

1. Tasha finds large **cities** fun.

2. Night makes the big **city** exciting.

3. She finds the bright **lights** pretty.

4. Shane, the chef, makes good **food** great.

5. He makes the chicken **stir-fry** spicy.

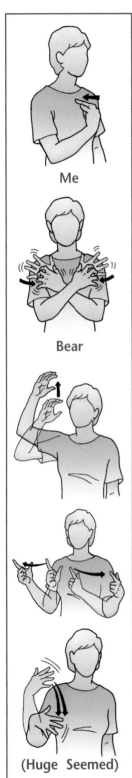

Me

Bear

(Huge Seemed)

You can write sentences with adjectives like those in Activity A. Follow these steps:

1. Choose a noun.
   Noun: student

2. Choose two or more adjectives to describe the noun.
   Adjectives: young, bright

3. Decide on a sentence pattern, and write the sentence.
   A subject + verb + d. object + adj. obj. complement
     Leslie called the young student bright.
   B subject + linking verb + adj. subj. complement
     The young student is bright.

Activity B On your paper, write a sentence for each group of words. Use an adjective object complement in five sentences (pattern **A** above). Use an adjective subject complement in the other five sentences (pattern **B** above).

1. snow, soft, cold

2. sun, bright, shiny

3. woman, careful, busy

4. car, old, broken

5. soccer player, active, quick

6. elephant, trained, strong

7. cat, fussy, hungry

8. boat, wooden, leaky

9. bike, loud, fast

10. student, smart, eager

To me, the bear seemed huge.

Some adjectives become adverbs when you add *-ly*.

EXAMPLE   **Adjectives**   quiet, soft, quick, noisy
                Adverbs   quietly, softly, quickly, noisily

To figure out whether a word is an adjective or an adverb, look carefully at the whole sentence. If the word comes right before a noun or follows a linking verb, it is probably an adjective. If the word ends in *-ly* and follows an action verb, it is probably an adverb.

Remember that an adjective always describes a noun. An adverb tells about a verb, an adjective, or another adverb.

EXAMPLE   **Adjective**   The child seems happy.
                (The linking verb *seems* links the adjective
                happy to the noun *child. Happy* is an adjective
                subject complement.)
                Adverb   The child plays happily.
                (The adverb *happily* answers the question *how*
                about the action verb *plays.*)

Activity A On your paper, write whether the word in bold is an *adjective* or an *adverb*. (You may wish to refer to the list of linking verbs in Lesson 3 on page 136.)

1. The birds in the park appeared **loud.**
2. The birds sang **loudly.**
3. It was a **happy** day for everyone.
4. The winter wind felt **brisk** and cold.
5. Mr. Stillman walked **briskly** to his car.

Activity B On your paper, write the word in parentheses that completes each of these sentences correctly. Next to the word, write whether it is an *adjective* or an *adverb*.

Example Al stacked boxes in a (neat, neatly) row.
      neat—adjective

   1. The (heavy, heavily) load shifted.

   2. The load fell (heavy, heavily) to the street.

   3. The boat moved (slow, slowly) out of the harbor.

   4. The skipper handled the sailboat (careful, carefully).

   5. Then a (strong, strongly) south wind moved the boat along (swift, swiftly).

The adjective *good* and the adverb *well* are often used incorrectly. Use *good* after a linking verb to describe the subject. Always use *good* to describe a noun or pronoun. Use *well* after an action verb to tell about the verb.

      Adjective   That movie was good.
                                 We ate a good dinner.
           Adverb   They ate well after their game.

Activity C Write each sentence on your paper. Fill in each blank with either *good* or *well* to complete each sentence correctly.

   1. That dress looks _____ on her.

   2. She slept _____ during the storm.

   3. The old house is in _____ shape.

   4. A cold drink tastes _____ on a hot day.

   5. Mateo works _____ under pressure.

Compound subject complement

Two or more subject complements joined by a conjunction

Sentences with subject complements may have compound parts and prepositional phrases. Two or more subject complements make a **compound subject complement.**

> EXAMPLE   On a hot summer afternoon, lipstick and cough drops in a warm car are messy, sticky, and runny.
>
> | **Compound subject** | lipstick, cough drops |
> | **Linking verb** | are |
> | **Compound subject complement** | messy, sticky, runny |

Although the example sentence has compound parts, adjectives, and prepositional phrases, it still follows the basic sentence pattern of *subject + linking verb + subject complement*. Remove the adjectives and prepositional phrases, and you can easily recognize the sentence pattern.

> EXAMPLE
>
> Lipstick and cough drops are messy, sticky, and runny.
>
>   *compound subject*   *verb*   *compound subject complement*

Activity A On your paper, write the subject complement in each sentence. Write whether the complement is a *noun subject complement* or an *adjective subject complement.*

1. Of all the town's cooks, Juan is the most talented chef.

2. For meats, Juan's own gravy recipe is a great one.

3. Over steaming rice, Juan's pepper beef stew with gravy and vegetables tastes spicy and terrific.

4. For a side dish, Juan's dinner rolls and salads of mixed greens are extremely fresh and tasty.

5. On Friday nights, Juan's restaurant in the city is full of happy diners.

Activity B On your paper, make a chart like the one shown. Write the words that form the basic sentence pattern in these sentences in the chart.

Example The student with top honors in medical school became a doctor and then chief of staff.

subject + linking verb + subject complement		
student	became	doctor, chief of staff

1. Most of the stores in town are bargain shops with good values at low cost.
2. The price of that blue coat in the store on Elm Street looks good to me.
3. The bus with the red sign was late on its way to the station.
4. The fine athlete is a major player on the team and a good student at his school in New York.
5. My brand new computer is a wonderful machine and a useful tool for almost any job.

Activity C Add adjectives, adverbs, compounds, and prepositional phrases to each sentence. Write the sentences on your paper.

1. Josh's car is a wreck.
2. The hood is dented.
3. Two windows are broken.
4. The tires appear flat.
5. That boy is an unhappy person.

Pronouns are often subjects of sentences with linking verbs. Here are examples of pronouns used as subjects with linking verbs.

it	that	these	this	those

EXAMPLE   This is a new song by your favorite singer.

Sentence pattern   subject + linking verb + subject complement

(The pronoun *this* is the subject of the sentence.)

Activity A Write each sentence on your paper. Write *S* above the subject pronoun, *LV* above the linking verb, and *NSC* above the noun subject complement.

                    S   LV   NSC
Example   Those were the best sheep on the farm.

1. This is the time for the picnic.

2. That is the dog with the sore foot.

3. These are the hottest months of the year.

4. That is a very common problem.

5. That was our last chance for help.

6. It was a neat deal.

7. This is a sea turtle from Florida.

8. It is an animal in trouble.

9. Those were my shoes in the box.

10. This is Leah's new telephone.

The adverbs *here* and *there* often appear first in sentences with linking verbs. To find the subject in sentences that begin with *here* or *there,* try turning the sentence around so that the noun or pronoun subject comes before the verb.

EXAMPLE	Here is the weekly magazine.
	There is the morning train.
	I I I I I
Parts of speech	*adv. verb adj. adj. noun*

To find the subjects, reverse the word order.

     The weekly magazine is here.
     The morning train is there.

Sentence pattern subject + verb

(The subject of the first sentence is *magazine.* The subject of the second sentence is *train.* The sentence pattern of the original sentences is *subject + verb* even though the order of the words is reversed.)

Activity B On your paper, write the subject of each sentence. If you have trouble finding the subject, try turning the sentence around. Two sentences have a compound subject.

1. There is a sailboat at the end of the lake.

2. Here is the key to the old chest.

3. There is a low, black car on the hilly road.

4. There are a herd of cattle and some sheep on the grassy hill.

5. There was a campfire near the lake.

6. There were bright flashes of lightning and loud cracks of thunder during the storm.

7. Here is a hot cup of coffee.

8. Here are the movie tickets to the next show.

9. There is a silver jet on the runway.

10. There was a moving van in front of his house.

You have learned that pronouns can take the place of nouns in a sentence.

Pronouns			
	Nominative	**Objective**	**Owner**
One	I	me	my, mine
	you	you	you, yours
	he, she, it	him, her, it	his, her, hers, its
Two or	we	us	our, ours
More	you	you	your, yours
	they	them	their, theirs

Use nominative pronouns as subjects and as subject complements in sentences with linking verbs. Use objective pronouns as direct objects and indirect objects in sentences with action verbs and as objects of prepositions.

EXAMPLE

Subject	I am happy.
Subject complement	It is I.
Direct object	Gabriel saw me.
Indirect object	Gabriel gave me a book.
Object of preposition	Gabriel gave a book to me.

Use owner pronouns as subject complements in sentences with linking verbs. These owner pronouns are

hers	his	its	mine	ours	theirs	yours

EXAMPLE

That chair is his.

	I	I	I	I
Parts of speech	adj.	n.	v.	pronoun
Sentence parts	subject | predicate			
Sentence pattern	subject + linking verb +			
	subject complement			

Activity A On your paper, write the correct pronoun in parentheses. Then write how each pronoun is used in the sentence.

Example   Elena gave (he, him) and (I, me) coupons for the restaurant.
            him, me—compound indirect object

1. (He, Him) and (I, me) sat together during the show.

2. Ahmad met (he, him) and (she, her) after the play.

3. The four of (we, us) ate at Jake's.

4. (He, Him) and (I, me) liked the play, but Cora did not.

5. The best tennis players are (he, him) and (she, her).

6. (Her, She) slams the ball across the net to (him, he).

7. The winners of the match are (they, them).

8. Afterward, (he, him) asked (she, her) for a ride home.

9. The waiter served lunch to (she, her) and (I, me).

10. The person in the picture is (she, her).

Activity B On your paper, write the second sentence of each set. Fill in the blank with an owner pronoun.

Example   Those dishes belong to me.
            They are <u>mine</u>.

1. Those clothes belong to Brigette. They are _____ .

2. Mr. and Mrs. Lee own the store. It is _____ .

3. That car belongs to Rob. It is _____ .

4. The books belong to you. They are _____ .

5. We own the table. It is _____ .

Remember, there are six sentence patterns.

Sentence Patterns
(1) subject + verb The salad chills.
(2) subject + verb + direct object The salad dressing stained the carpet.
(3) subject + verb + indirect object + direct object He served her a salad.
(4) subject + verb + direct object + object complement I find this salad tasty.
(5) subject + linking verb + noun subject complement This salad is a healthy choice.
(6) subject + linking verb + adjective subject complement The salad is big.

Activity A Write each sentence on your paper. Fill in the blank with a word of your own choosing.

Example   Soccer is my favorite _____<u>sport</u>_____ .
                                  noun subject complement

1. _____ smiled.
           subject

2. Rose gave _____ a present.
                  indirect object

3. Carol watched a _____ .
                        direct object

4. This CD is _____ .
              adjective subject complement

5. One girl called the concert _____ .
                                   object complement

Activity B Identify the correct sentence pattern for each sentence. On your paper, write the number that matches one of the sentence patterns from the chart on page 148.

Example   The group of students opened their textbooks to the lesson on sentence patterns.
2 (subject + verb + direct object)

1. Todd was late again.

2. Ms. Costa turned to the class and asked the students a question.

3. Steven gave the right answer.

4. Steven felt smart, and he was proud of himself.

5. He smiled happily.

6. Then she taught the class another grammar lesson.

7. Ms. Costa is a good English teacher.

8. Most students thought the lesson an easy one.

9. Several began their work.

10. Ms. Costa allowed them ten minutes.

11. Everyone finished on time.

12. Well, Todd was a little slow with his paper.

13. Later, the teacher corrected the papers quickly.

14. After school, Todd offered Gina a ride home.

15. Todd's old car is a rare model.

Ms. Costa answers Todd's question.

You know that a sentence is a group of words arranged in a certain pattern to express an idea. You and a friend may start with the same list of words, but you will probably write totally different sentences that express different ideas. Your choice of words and how you arrange them will create a different picture in a reader's mind than your friend's sentence will.

Look at the following list of words. Think about an idea for a sentence using some of these words. Then compare your idea with other students' ideas.

Subjects	Adjectives	Subject Complements
morning	bright	gloomy
evening	dark	one
	new	
	starry	
	lovely	

Activity A Using the list of subjects, adjectives, and subject complements below, write five clear sentences using linking verbs on your paper. Add other words as needed.

Subjects	Adjectives	Noun and Adjective Subject Complements
sandwich	tangy	cheap
vegetables	cold	one
orange	hot	dinner
juice	crispy	great
lasagna	juicy	drink

Activity B Improve the sentences you wrote in Activity A by adding adverbs and prepositional phrases. Write your revised sentences on your paper.

Activity C Use the sentences from Activity B to write a short story about food. Proofread and edit your story.

Activity D Use the list of subjects, adjectives, and subject complements below to write on your paper five clear sentences using linking verbs. Add other adjectives as needed.

Subjects	Adjectives	Noun and Adjective Subject Complements
spider	cute	angry
tiger	hairy	pet
cat	scary	beast
elephant	toothy	noisy
gorilla	strong	huge

Activity E Improve the sentences you wrote in Activity D by adding adverbs and prepositional phrases. Write your revised sentences on your paper.

Activity F Use the sentences from Activity E to write a short story about zoo animals. Proofread and edit your story.

Activity G Now it's your turn. Think about a topic: for example, cars, sports, movies, music, computer games, or anything else that interests you. Next, make a list of words that you might use to describe your topic. You might wish to list the words in a chart similar to the charts shown in this lesson. Finally, follow the steps in the writing process to write a short story on your topic.

Comparative
An adjective that compares two nouns

Superlative
An adjective that compares three or more nouns

Adjectives compare people, places, and things. When you compare two things, the adjective usually has an *-er* added to it. **Comparatives** are adjectives that compare two things. When you compare more than two things, the adjective usually has an *-est* added to it. **Superlatives** are adjectives that compare more than two things.

Writing Tip

Beware of double comparisons. Do not add *more* or *most* when you use the *-er* or *-est* form of an adjective.

EXAMPLE

Mariah is	Of the two, Ines is	Of the three, Estella is
quick	quicker	quickest
tall	taller	tallest
early	earlier	earliest
hungry	hungrier	hungriest
happy	happier	happiest

Some adjectives change completely to form their comparative and superlative forms.

EXAMPLE

Adjective	Comparative	Superlative
bad	worse	worst
good	better	best
little	less	least
many	more	most

Activity A On your paper, write the correct form of the adjective in parentheses for each sentence.

1. Javier is the (faster, fastest) runner on the whole team.
2. Of the two comics, she is the (funnier, funniest).
3. Coco is the (fatter, fattest) cat on the block.
4. Sophie is the (taller, tallest) student in her class.
5. Maria is the (older, oldest) of the two sisters.

Bad

Worse

Good

Better

Activity B On your paper, write the correct form of the adjective in parentheses for each sentence.

1. Of the mother and daughter, the daughter is (tallest, taller).

2. The pig is the (smarter, smartest) of all the animals in that story.

3. My test scores are high, but Jeff's are (higher, highest).

4. Tela's computer is fast, but Maiya's computer is (fastest, faster).

5. That store carries the (fresher, freshest) vegetables of any store in town.

Activity C On your paper, write the correct form of the adjective in parentheses for each sentence.

1. Many people find her the (more, most) talented of all stage actors.

2. In all the family, she is (more, most) famous.

3. Of the two sisters, her acting is (better, best).

4. Her singing is (worse, bad), but she has the (best, better) voice of all the sisters.

5. Of the two problems, this is (less, least) difficult.

6. It is my (least, less) favorite of all.

7. My grades are (good, better), but yours are (best, better).

8. Of the five team members, Pauline has scored the (more, most) points.

9. The Eagles had a bad season, but the Blazers had the (worse, worst) record in the league.

10. Of the two teams, their record is (worse, worst).

Using What You've Learned

Write five sentences comparing two or more movies, TV programs, or books. Compare the items with adjectives. When you have finished writing, check to make sure that you have used the correct comparative or superlative form of each adjective.

Word Bank

adjective subject complement

comparative

compound subject complement

linking verb

noun subject complement

subject complement

superlative

Part A   Read each sentence below. Fill in each blank with a vocabulary word that correctly completes each sentence.

1. Two or more subject complements make a _____ .

2. A _____ is a word in the predicate renaming the subject.

3. A word in the predicate describing the subject is a _____ .

4. A verb connecting the subject to a word in the predicate is a _____ .

5. A _____ compares more than two things.

6. An adjective in the predicate describing the subject is an _____ .

7. An adjective that compares two things is a _____ .

Part B   Read this paragraph.

Devon's truck is good for long trips. His truck carries heavy loads. Two of Devon's friends are his partners. They split the costs of each trip. Truck travel pays well for all of them. Devon feels proud that he owns a truck.

Find these words in the paragraph. Match them with the correct labels. On your paper, write the numbers and letters.

Words	Labels
8. They	**A** linking verb
9. partners	**B** adjective subject complement
10. well	**C** pronoun as a subject
11. feels	**D** pronoun as an object of a preposition
12. good	**E** noun subject complement
13. them	**F** adverb

Part C   Write the adjectives that describe the nouns in bold.

14. In the park, the **trees** are huge.

15. He finds the large **statues** interesting.

16. On weekends, the **crowds** seem large.

17. There is a cafe that serves the **food** hot.

Part D Write the word in parentheses that correctly completes each of these sentences.

18. People drive (quick, quickly) on this road.

19. (He, Him) and (I, me) drive together in the morning.

20. Later, (her, she) asked (he, him) for a ride.

21. Rush hour is the (worse, worst) time of day for traffic.

22. That street has (bad, worse) potholes, but the potholes on this street are (worse, worst).

23. Several of (we, us) rode the bus.

24. Choose (good, well) words, and use them (good, well).

Part E Choose the owner pronoun that correctly completes each set of sentences.

25. Jason owns the computer. It is _____ .

    A him's   **B** he's   **C** his   **D** him

26. The newspaper belongs to the club members. It is _____ .

    A there's   **B** theirs   **C** them's   **D** their

27. Perla owns these videos. They are _____ .

    A hers'   **B** her's   **C** her   **D** hers

Part F Identify and write on your paper the sentence pattern for each of these sentences. Look back at the list of sentence patterns and example sentences in Lesson 9 on page 148 for help. Underline any linking verbs.

28. His dogs are healthy.

29. Terry and Jamilla are good friends.

30. Patrick bought her a ticket to the rodeo.

Test-Taking Tip Read test questions carefully to identify those questions that require more than one answer.

8

Verbs Tell Time

How important is it to know when something happened or is going to happen? For example, timing is important in nature. As things grow, they have a past, a present, and a future. This photograph shows some stages in a tree's growth. In the past, the tree grew buds, and the buds bloomed. Now—in the present—the tree has apples on it. You can predict what will happen to the apple tree in the future. Birds and people might eat the apples. Maybe the apples will fall to the ground.

Sentences also indicate time. Readers want to know when something happened. The verb in a sentence tells whether something happened in the past, whether it is happening now, or whether it will happen in the future.

In this chapter, you will learn how verbs can tell time in your own writing. You will practice using verbs to indicate when something happened.

Goals for Learning

◆ To use verbs in past, present, and future forms

◆ To use helping verbs and negative adverbs

◆ To use correct forms of irregular verbs

◆ To identify and use contractions

Tense

Present, past, or future time expressed by a verb

Regular verb

A verb that adds -d or -ed to form the past tense

Verbs show action or a state-of-being. An action verb tells what the subject of a sentence is doing. Linking, or state-of-being, verbs link the subject to nouns or adjectives in the predicate. Linking verbs help the predicate tell more about the subject.

Activity A On your paper, write the verb in each sentence. Next to each verb, write whether it is an *action verb* or a *linking verb*.

1. The wet streets shine under the light.

2. Francisco works the late shift.

3. He seems really sick today.

4. Andy feels awful, too.

5. Both men left work early.

There are six verb tenses in all:
- present
- past
- future
- present perfect
- past perfect
- future perfect

A verb's **tense** refers to the period of time expressed by the verb. The tense of a verb tells you whether something

- happened in the past

- is happening in the present, or

- will happen in the future.

Regular verbs form their past tense by adding *-d* or *-ed* at the end. Add *-d* to regular verbs that end in *-e*. Add *-ed* to regular verbs that end in other letters.

EXAMPLE		
Present	Today, I smile.
Past	Yesterday, I smiled.
Future	Tomorrow, I will smile.
Present	Today, I walk.
Past	Yesterday, I walked.
Future	Tomorrow, I will walk.

Smile

(Smile + Finish) Smiled

(Smile + Will) Will Smile

Activity B On your paper, write the verbs in these sentences. (Include the word *will* with future tense verbs.) Write whether the verb is in the *present, past,* or *future* tense.

1. Yesterday, I changed schools.
2. Today, I talk with my teacher.
3. Yesterday, I started class.
4. Tomorrow, I will learn about verbs.
5. Yesterday, I learned about sentences.
6. Yesterday, I jumped rope.
7. Tomorrow, I will play basketball with my friends.
8. Today, I watch TV at home.
9. Yesterday, you looked sad about something.
10. Today, you appear fine.

Activity C Complete each sentence using the bold verb in the tense given in parentheses. Write the sentence on your paper. Each of the verbs given is a regular verb.

Example The dogs _____ louder than usual.
(**bark**, past tense)
The dogs **barked** louder than usual.

1. Lin _____ quite happy about her test grade.
(**seem**, past tense)
2. The sauce _____ quite spicy. (**taste**, past tense)
3. The girls _____ about their plans for the summer.
(**talk**, future tense)
4. I _____ for a happy ending to the story.
(**wish**, past tense)
5. She _____ the steps for the directions in order.
(**list**, future tense)

A **helping verb** is a verb that comes before the main verb. A helping verb *helps* the main verb show action or state a fact. A main verb with one or more helping verbs is a **verb phrase.**

Helping verb
A verb that comes before the main verb. Together, the two verbs form a verb phrase

Verb phrase
A verb and its helpers

> **EXAMPLE**   I was dreaming.
> He could be dreaming.
> You must have been dreaming.
>
> (In each of the verb phrases, *dreaming* is the main verb. *Was, could, be, must, have,* and *been* are all helping verbs.)

Forms of the verbs *be, have,* and *do* often serve as helping verbs. Here is a list of common helping verbs:

am	can	doing	is	should
are	could	had	may	was
be	did	has	might	were
been	do	have	must	will
being	does	having	shall	would

Verbs in the future tense always use a helping verb.

> **EXAMPLE**   Megan **will go** to the movies later.
>
> (The verb phrase *will go* consists of the main verb *go* and the helping verb *will.*)

Activity A On your paper, write the bold verb phrase in each sentence. Draw one line under the main verb. Circle the helping verb.

1. Hannah **has packed** her bags.
2. She **will be leaving** tomorrow.
3. Steve and his friends **are listening** to music.
4. They **have been looking** for information about Braille.
5. Kerry **did read** a book in Braille.

Communication Connection

In the Braille system, raised dots represent letters, combinations of letters, numbers, and punctuation marks. People learn Braille by remembering what each group of dots stands for, just as people with sight learn the alphabet. The word *Braille* written in Braille looks like this:

The perfect tenses use a helping verb with a past form of the verb.

Present perfect
I have packed.

Past perfect
I had packed.

Future perfect
I will have packed.

Activity B On your paper, write the verb phrase in each sentence. Draw one line under the main verb. Circle the helping verb.

1. David will earn extra money at his job.

2. Then he can buy a Mother's Day gift.

3. The store does deliver gifts for its best customers.

4. The gift should surprise David's mother.

5. Probably she will be smiling happily all day.

6. Pamela did go to the dentist.

7. Her brother must visit the dentist, too.

8. They could have been checked at the same time.

9. Pamela has been taking good care of her teeth.

10. The dentist will praise her.

Activity C Complete each sentence with a verb phrase. Use the verb in parentheses and one or more helping verbs from the list on page 160. Write the completed sentences on your paper.

Example   Ben, a grain and cattle farmer, _____ hard. (work)
Ben, a grain and cattle farmer, has been working hard.

1. He _____ many acres of corn. (plant)

2. He _____ his corn in that tall silo. (store)

3. He _____ some of his corn to his cattle. (feed)

4. Ben _____ his fields carefully. (tend)

5. Ben _____ on his farm for a long time. (live)

6. Luisa _____ the most beautiful quilt by hand. (stitch)

7. She _____ her quilt at the fair. (show)

8. She _____ it in the craft contest. (enter)

9. Her quilt _____ the first prize. (award)

10. Luisa certainly _____ proud of her skills as a quilter. (feel)

Verbs that tell about action that takes place now or continues to take place are in the **present tense.** There are four present tense verb forms.

EXAMPLE

Emily plays soccer.
Emily is playing on a team.
Emily has played well all season.
Emily has been playing soccer for three years.

The helping verbs for present tense are *am, is, are, have, has, has been,* and *have been.*

EXAMPLE

I am running.   You have run.
He is running.   She has run.
They are running.   We have been running.

Activity A Number your paper from 1 to 4. Rewrite the following sentence four times. Each time, use a different form of the present tense for the verb *wait.*

Hulk, the dog, _____ for a bone.

Verbs must agree with their subjects. Many verbs add an -*s* or -*es* to their present tense form when the subject of a sentence is singular.

EXAMPLE

Singular subject   Aram looks.   He watches.
Plural subject   Aram and Joe look.   They watch.

In sentences with verb phrases, the helping verbs must agree with the subjects.

EXAMPLE

Singular subject   Juanita does look.   She is watching.
Plural subject   I do look.   We are watching.

Never use *be* as a helping verb in present tense verbs. Never use *been* alone as a helping verb or as a main verb. Use *has* or *have* with *been*.

EXAMPLE **Incorrect** They be waiting for a letter.
Correct They are waiting for a letter.

Incorrect They been waiting for a month.
Correct They have been waiting for a month.

Activity B Write these sentences using the correct present tense forms of the verbs.

1. I be going to the street fair.
2. They am going with me.
3. I been walking down the road.
4. We has been talking with friends.
5. Danny am shopping at the store.
6. He be shopping with her.
7. We is riding the bus uptown.
8. Terri been sitting by the window.
9. We was working all evening.
10. She am studying for a test.
11. I been looking out the window.
12. They is looking for a place to live.
13. Michiko and Tim has been driving all night.
14. She be in class all day.
15. Joe work at the gas station.

Past tense

The verb tense that tells about action in the past

Verbs that tell about action that happened in the past are in the **past tense.** There are four past tense verb forms.

> **EXAMPLE**
> Emily played soccer.
> Emily was playing well.
> Emily had played many times.
> Emily had been playing goalie.

The helping verbs for past tense are *was, were, had,* and *had been.*

> **EXAMPLE**
> I was running.   You were running.
> She had run.   They had been running.

Activity A Number your paper from 1 to 4. Rewrite the following sentence four times. Each time, use a different form of the past tense for the verb *wait.*

> Hulk, the dog, _____ for a bone.

Use the correct form of the helping verb *be* in past tense verbs. Remember that a singular subject takes a singular form of the verb. *You* is always a plural subject.

> **EXAMPLE**
> **Singular subject**   I was looking.
>   He was watching.
> **Plural subject**   You were looking.
>   Holly and Kentaro were watching.

Do not use *done* as a helping verb in past tense verbs. The combination *done been* is never correct. Use the helping verb *had* with *been* in past tense verbs.

EXAMPLE	Incorrect	They done waited for a month.
	Correct	They waited for a month.
	Correct	They were waiting for a month.
	Incorrect	They done been waiting for a letter.
	Correct	They had been waiting for a letter.

Activity B Write these sentences using the correct past tense forms of the verbs.

1. They was heading for home.
2. They had done fished all day.
3. I were fishing, too.
4. We was talking about movies.
5. Ellen been walking with her folks.
6. I been waiting for them.
7. I done helped them.
8. Lucy have bowled a perfect game.
9. Jeff been working at the post office.
10. You was waiting at the station.
11. They had done been gone since yesterday.
12. We been waiting for you.
13. He done seen that video three times.
14. The girls was swimming in the pool.
15. I were helping Brad load the truck.

Future tense

The verb tense that tells about action in the future

Verbs that tell about action that has not yet happened are in the **future tense.** There are four future tense verb forms.

EXAMPLE Emily will play soccer again.
Emily will be playing hard.
Emily will have played more games.
Emily will have been playing goalie all season.

Writing Tip

You can also use the phrases *about to* and *going to* to tell about action in the future. Just combine the phrase with a form of *be* and a verb.

Example I am about to leave. I am going to play.

All forms of verbs in the future tense need the helping verb *will*. Some future forms need other helping verbs, too. The helping verbs for future tense are *will, will be, will have,* and *will have been.*

EXAMPLE I will run.
She will have run.
You will be running.
They will have been running.

Activity A Number your paper from 1 to 4. Rewrite the following sentence four times. Each time, use a different form of the future tense for the verb *wait.*

Hulk, the dog, _____ for a bone.

Never use *be* as a helping verb in future tense verbs. Always use *will have* with *been* in future tense verbs.

EXAMPLE
Incorrect The bus be coming soon.
Correct The bus will be coming soon.

Incorrect In a few days, they been waiting for a month.
Correct In a few days, they will have been waiting for a month.

B

U

S

Soon

Coming

Will

The bus will be
coming soon.

Activity B Write these sentences using the correct future tense forms of the verbs. Remember that all verbs in future tense use the helping verb *will*.

1. Brenda and Sam be doing well.
2. I be doing well next year.
3. The whole group be needing some food.
4. Everyone eating really well.
5. We be working with him.
6. Her car be needing new tires soon.
7. They work hard next year.
8. The dark clouds drop rain later this afternoon.
9. Stan be taking three tests tomorrow.
10. Midori work nights next week.
11. He be sorry tomorrow.
12. Mike be doing better in school next year.
13. I be ready for anything next week.
14. We be early for school tomorrow.
15. Jane be planning a surprise for her friend Chris.

Negative

A word that means "no" or "not" and that stops the action of the verb

A **negative** is a word that means "no" or "not." Negatives, such as *not* and *never*, often come between the helping verb and the main verb in a verb phrase. Negatives may go with present, past, and future tense verb forms.

EXAMPLE

Present tense	Oliva is *not* giving guitar lessons this summer.
Past tense	We had *never* met our new coach.
Future tense	She will *not* know our names.

(The verb phrase in each example sentence is in color. *Not* and *never* are adverbs. *Not* and *never* are never part of a verb phrase.)

Activity A Write these sentences on your paper. Underline the verb phrases in the sentences. Circle the negatives.

1. The storm will not be blowing from the east.

2. They will never walk on the beach again.

3. The waves had not covered the whole beach.

4. Waves have not been smashing against the shore for very long.

5. The stores near the beach were not opening their doors.

6. Many people will not forget that awful storm.

7. John has never gone to the beach before, and he has not seen a big storm on the coast.

8. The storm has not arrived yet, but it will not cause much damage.

9. People will not pull their boats from the water.

10. This coast will never be the same.

Activity B Add *not* or *never* to the verbs in these sentences. Write the sentences on your paper. Underline the verb phrases. Then write whether the verb is in *present tense*, *past tense*, or *future tense*.

Example   The lighthouse had been warning ships about the rocks.

The lighthouse <u>had</u> not <u>been warning</u> ships about the rocks.—past tense

1. Small houses are clustered around the lighthouse.
2. The keeper of the lighthouse is living there.
3. He has been staying in the lighthouse most nights.
4. He will have lived near the lighthouse for seven years.
5. She will hold the meeting here.
6. Others will be coming to her office for the meeting.
7. She will make a deal.
8. She will be building the new place in another six months.
9. Phil and his horse are riding in many events of the rodeo.
10. His horse has jumped over barrels.
11. Phil had roped calves.
12. Phil had won prizes at the rodeo.
13. Alfredo has been using his computer every day.
14. He is playing video games with his friends.
15. This computer will solve all of Alfredo's problems.

The lighthouse stands on the shore.

Irregular verb

A verb that changes its form to form past tenses

You have learned that regular verbs form their past tense by adding *-d* or *-ed* to their present form. Some regular verbs such as *burn* and *dream* can also add *-t* to form their past tense.

EXAMPLE

Present tense	burn	dream
Past tense	burned or burnt	dreamed or dreamt

Irregular verbs do not add *-d* or *-ed* to form their past tenses. They form their tenses in other ways. Study this list of irregular verbs. These verbs do not follow any pattern. The only way that you can remember their different forms is to memorize them.

Present	Past	With a Helping Verb
break	broke	(has) broken
bend	bent	(has) bent
burst	burst	(has) burst
catch	caught	(has) caught
come	came	(has) come
drink	drank	(has) drunk
drive	drove	(has) driven
eat	ate	(has) eaten
know	knew	(has) known
ride	rode	(has) ridden
run	ran	(has) run
see	saw	(has) seen
spring	sprang	(has) sprung
swim	swam	(has) swum
take	took	(has) taken
throw	threw	(has) thrown
write	wrote	(has) written

Activity A On your paper, write the correct form of each verb in these sentences. Then write whether the verb is *present tense, past tense,* or *future tense.*

1. The three friends have never _____ out to the island. (swim)

2. They _____ some practice laps yesterday. (swim)

3. Sharon will not _____ to the lake with us. (come)

4. The friends have _____ many large fish in that lake. (catch)

5. Over the years, much bait has been _____ into the lake. (throw)

6. The cowboys must have _____ the cattle across the ranch. (drive)

7. They had _____ long and hard for weeks. (ride)

8. At camp, Frank has _____ one calf to the ground. (throw)

9. A cowboy's life has always _____ a lot of hard work. (take)

10. Yesterday, Frank _____ his rope around many cattle. (throw)

11. Next time, we will _____ it in a bucket. (catch)

12. Rita had never _____ anyone as talented as her dance teacher. (know)

13. Rita has _____ of dancing in Broadway shows. (dream)

14. She had _____ her leg badly as a young child. (broke)

15. Afterward, she _____ dancing lessons for therapy. (take)

Students in the dance class practice their steps.

Your writing should create images in the minds of others. A good writer can make readers think they are taking part in the story.

Activity A Write a children's story about a dragon. Have your story take place in the past. Follow the four steps in the writing process.

1. **Prewrite.** Think about stories that children enjoy. Think about dragons, and pretend they really did exist sometime in the past.

> **List words to describe the dragon. Ask:**
> Is the dragon friendly? clumsy? brave or not? Does it have a funny tail? fiery breath? Does it laugh? giggle? growl?

2. **Write.** Give your dragon a name. Write about what it saw and where it went. Write about what it did. Use your list of describing words.

> **Example of a beginning:**
> howard was a sily dragon with a funny tail. he meets a little boy who wanted a ride.

3. **Rewrite.** Look at what you wrote. Would a young child enjoy your story? Is it exciting? funny? scary? Can you make it more interesting?

> **Example of a beginning rewrite:**
> Once upon a time, a very sily dragon named howard meets a little boy. the boy looks at the big dragon and says in a small brave voice may I have a ride.

4. **Edit.** Check to make sure that the verbs are all in the past tense. Check for spelling, end marks, and commas.

Review a classmate's story. Do the verbs agree in number with their subjects? Are negatives correct? Are past forms of irregular verbs correct? Give suggestions for corrections. Share ideas about other ways to improve the story.

Example of an edited beginning:
Once upon a time, a very silly dragon named Howard met a little boy. The boy looked at the big dragon and said in a small, brave voice, "May I have a ride?"

Activity B Write a story about something that is happening right now. Follow the steps of the writing process.

1. **Prewrite.** Think about a man driving a car, a woman working, or a child playing a game. Choose one of these people to be the main character in your story.

2. **Write.** Write about what the person is doing now. Where is the person? What's happening? Is the person happy or sad? laughing or crying? running or sitting? eating or sleeping? What will happen to the person by the end of the story?

3. **Rewrite.** Read your story. Is it interesting? Can you improve it? Try to make it better.

4. **Edit.** Look at the verbs you wrote. The story happens in the present time. Are your verbs all in present tense? Check spelling, end marks, and commas.

Activity C Write a story that takes place in the future. Follow the steps of the writing process.

1. **Prewrite.** Think about ways people will travel in the future. Think about spaceships. Pretend a spaceship will take tourists to Jupiter.

2. **Write.** Write about a trip to Jupiter. Who will be on the trip? What funny or scary things will happen on the way?

3. **Rewrite.** Read your story. Is it exciting? Can you make it more interesting? Rewrite sentences to improve your story.

4. **Edit.** Look at the verbs you wrote. Your story takes place in the future. Are your verbs correct? Check spelling, end marks, and commas.

Contraction

A word formed when two words are put together and letters are left out

A **contraction** is one word made from two words. A contraction needs an apostrophe. Remember that an apostrophe is a punctuation mark. It takes the place of letters that you leave out when you form a contraction.

EXAMPLE   let + us = let's   Let's go swimming.
that + is = that's   That's a good idea.

A pronoun + a helping verb:
I + am = I'm
you + are = you're
we + are = we're
they + are = they're
she, he, it + is = she's, he's, it's

I + will = I'll
you + will = you'll
we + will = we'll
they + will = they'll
she, he, it + will = she'll, he'll, it'll

I + have = I've
you + have = you've
we + have = we've
they + have = they've

I + would = I'd
you + would = you'd
we + would = we'd
they + would = they'd
she, he, it + would = she'd, he'd, it'd

A verb + the adverb *not*:
are + not = aren't
were + not = weren't
has + not = hasn't
is + not = isn't
do + not = don't
does + not = doesn't
did + not = didn't
will + not = won't
could + not = couldn't
would + not = wouldn't
should + not = shouldn't

Find *will + not* on the chart on page 174. Notice that the contraction *won't* does not follow the usual pattern for forming contractions. Remember *will + not = won't*.

Activity A On your paper, write the contractions in these sentences correctly.

1. Its here somewhere.

2. Ive lost it, and its not on the table now.

3. Shell look on that other table for me.

4. It couldnt just walk away.

5. Ill find it soon, and I wont lose it again.

Activity B Change each pair of underlined words to a contraction. Write the contractions on your paper.

1. He is having a problem and does not know it.

2. He should not lose things.

3. You are going to keep track of your papers.

4. He did not find that last sheet of paper.

5. He has not looked in the desk, and that is where it is.

Activity C Match the words with their meanings. Write the number and its correct letter on your paper.

Words	Meanings
1. present	**A** yesterday
2. past	**B** tomorrow
3. future	**C** helping verb plus main verb
4. contraction	**D** today
5. verb phrase	**E** needs an apostrophe

Chapter 8   R E V I E W

Word Bank

contraction

future tense

helping verb

irregular verb

negative

past tense

present tense

regular verb

tense

verb phrase

Part A Use the words from the Word Bank to complete sentences 1–10.

1. The tense that tells about action in the present is _____ .
2. A _____ is a verb and its helpers.
3. A _____ is a word that means "no" or "not."
4. A verb that adds *-d* or *-ed* to form the past tense is a _____ .
5. The present, past, or future time expressed by a verb is its _____ .
6. The tense that tells about action in the future is _____ .
7. A _____ is one word made from two words.
8. An _____ changes its form in the past tense.
9. The tense that tells about action in the past is _____ .
10. A _____ is a verb that comes before the main verb.

Part B On your paper, write the verb phrase in each sentence. Label it *past*, *present*, or *future*. Circle the helping verbs, and underline the main verbs.

11. The trip had begun miles away and months ago.
12. Adam has been going through wild country.
13. The wagon will have broken down many times.
14. Heat and cold have given him a bad time.

Part C Write the correct form of each verb in parentheses.

15. By tonight, Adam will have _____ late. (ride)
16. He will have _____ by the campfire. (eat)
17. His mules will have _____ from a stream. (drink)
18. During the day, Adam will _____ many things. (see)

Part D Write the correct present tense form of each verb.

19. Ted (make) phone calls from his desk.
20. By the end of the season, Ted (use) his large machines.
21. Each machine (cost) a lot of money.
22. One machine (feed) his cattle, while another (weigh) them.

Part E Number your paper from 23 to 26. Change all the verbs in Part D to past tense. Add helping verbs as needed.

Part F Number your paper from 27 to 30. Change all the verbs in Part D to future tense. Add helping verbs as needed.

Part G Add *not* or *never* to change the meaning of these sentences. Label each verb *action* or *linking*.

31. Denzel has been there.

32. It was fun.

33. Jane does like the place.

34. You will enjoy it.

35. My friends are there.

Part H Write these sentences correctly on your paper.

36. sometimes edna cant find the trail

37. she doesnt have a map

38. he doesnt have the energy left

39. we dont have a camp for the night

Part I Write these sentences correctly on your paper. Form contractions with the underlined words.

40. the tent <u>will not</u> stay up

41. oh <u>it is</u> raining hard now

42. this trip <u>has not</u> been fun

Part J Write the letter of the correct word or group of words.

43. The football player _____ find his helmet.

   A couldnt   **B** couldn't   **C** could'nt   **D** coudn't

44. My favorite store at the mall _____ a sale next week.

   A will have   **B** has had   **C** will had   **D** had

45. The teacher had _____ the class on a field trip.

   A took   **B** tooken   **C** taked   **D** taken

Test-Taking Tip If you will have to define terms on a test, write each term on one side of a card. Write its definition on the other. Then test yourself, or work with a partner.

Be Exact

Have you ever looked closely at stained glass windows? They are made of hundreds of tiny pieces of glass that fit together perfectly to form an image. People who make stained glass windows must have the skill and the patience to fit the pieces of glass together like pieces of a puzzle.

Creating a stained glass window requires precision—using exactly the right piece in exactly the right spot. Similarly, it is important to use exact language when we speak and write. If we know exactly the right words to use, our ideas will be clear and easy to understand: our readers won't have to "fill in the blanks" to imagine what we meant.

In this chapter you will study ways to be more exact when you speak and write.

Goals for Learning

◆ To practice journal writing and note-taking

◆ To choose between easily confused words such as *accept/except* and *lie/lay*

◆ To use correctly words that sound alike but have different spellings

◆ To correct sentences with double negatives

◆ To practice writing a comparison and contrast paragraph

◆ To use correctly abbreviations for time of day and year

179

Writing Tip

When you take notes, try to use your own words. Putting what you read in your own words is especially important if you plan to use your notes to write a report.

Have you ever seen an interesting looking person and thought he or she would make a great story character? Have you ever heard a joke and said to yourself, "I should write that down so I don't forget it"? Writing your ideas in a journal is one way to record your thoughts and preserve important memories. You can use any kind of notebook for a journal. Write in it as often as you like.

Activity A On your paper, practice writing a journal entry. Use these ideas.

- Put today's date on the top of the page.
- Write about the best part of today.
- Write about the worst part of today.
- Describe something you saw today in as much detail as you can recall. It can be anything—a bird in its nest, a dark rain cloud, a person you passed on the street.

When you want to remember facts and details from class, you can take notes. Notes should include the most important words and ideas. In order to be helpful, reminder notes need to be complete. They also should be neat enough to read and understand.

Activity B On your paper, write reminder notes using only important words from each sentence.

Example   Abraham Lincoln, one of the wisest leaders of this country, was the sixteenth president.
Abraham Lincoln—16th president

1. In 1861, he became president of the United States during a time of trouble between the states.

2. His leadership during the Civil War made Lincoln famous.

3. Lincoln wanted all people to be free.

4. He signed a paper and gave African slaves their freedom.

5. People called him foolish, but he won the war.

Activity C Write the letter of the note that has more information in each set on your paper. Then use the information in that note to write a more exact sentence.

1. Mary has an appointment.

A. dentist

B. dentist— 8 a.m. Thursday, May 5

2. Paul has an errand to do.

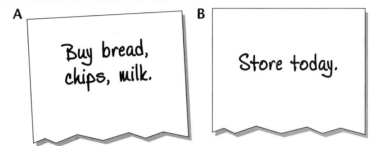

A. Buy bread, chips, milk.

B. Store today.

3. Sasha is going downtown.

A. Meet a friend in front of store this afternoon.

B. Meet Trina — 4 p.m. at 306 Walnut.

Writing Tip

The word *accept* sometimes means "to agree to."

If you have to respond in writing to an invitation, use *accept*, not *except*.

People often confuse the words *accept* and *except*. *Accept* is a verb that means "to take" or "to receive."

EXAMPLE   Guadalupe will accept the call.

Except can be a verb that means "to leave out." It can also be a preposition that means "but."

EXAMPLE

Verb	My father was happy all day, if you except the early morning.
Preposition	No one likes mornings except my mother.

Activity A On your paper, write the word in parentheses that completes each sentence correctly.

1. The teacher will (except, accept) Sam's answers on the test.

2. He answered all the questions correctly (except, accept) three in the math section.

3. All of the students (except, accept) Sam did well in math.

4. Sam will have to (except, accept) a grade of C.

5. He likes school (except, accept) for math.

People sometimes mix up the verbs *learn* and *teach*. *Teach* means "to give new facts." *Learn* means "to get new facts."

EXAMPLE   Yolanda teaches history to Felipe.
(Yolanda is giving facts.)
Felipe learns history from Yolanda.
(Felipe is getting facts.)

Activity B On your paper, write the word in parentheses that completes each sentence correctly.

1. The booklet will (teach, learn) David a skill.

2. David (taught, learned) a skill from the booklet.

3. Mr. Santos (taught, learned) Peter the violin for three years.

4. I will (teach, learn) you how to play the flute.

5. Lisa will (teach, learn) Ricky some songs.

Activity C On your paper, write the word in parentheses that completes each sentence correctly.

1. Clem (learned, taught) piano to all his sisters (accept, except) the littlest one.

2. Bill will (accept, except) payment from everyone (accept, except) Sara.

3. Those students (learned, taught) every subject from Mr. Adams (accept, except) science.

4. Everyone (accept, except) Tom (learned, taught) something from that last defeat.

5. The bank clerk (accepted, excepted) checks from every student (accept, except) Myra.

Selecting accurate verbs takes practice.

Many people confuse these words: *their, there,* and *they're; your* and *you're; its* and *it's. Their, your,* and *its* are owner pronouns. They do not have apostrophes. *They're, you're,* and *it's* are contractions. Contractions do have apostrophes.

Owner Pronouns	Contractions		Adverb
their	they're	= they are	there
your	you're	= you are	
its	it's	= it is	

There is an adverb that tells where an action takes place.

EXAMPLE   We can walk there after practice.

Activity A On your paper, write the words in parentheses that complete the sentences correctly.

1. Andy pulled his boat into (their, they're, there) dock.

2. Twin pipes gurgled beneath (its, it's) stern.

3. (Its, It's) a fast one, and (your, you're) lucky.

4. (Their, They're, There) here to see (your, you're) boat.

5. The boat cost more than (their, they're, there) house.

6. (Their, They're, There) go (your, you're) cousin Jessie and her sister.

7. (Their, They're, There) cruising in (their, they're, there) new car.

8. (Their, They're, There) having a great time with (you're, your) friend Emma.

9. (Your, You're) going (their, they're, there) with them later.

10. (Their, They're, There) is math homework on (your, you're) desk.

You can use the word *there* with a form of the verb *to be* at the beginning of a sentence.

Example
There is the book.

The words *there* and *is* can form the contraction *there's.*

Example
There's the book.

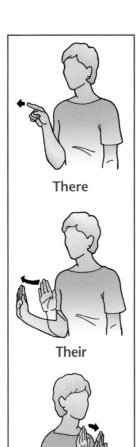

There

Their

Your

Activity B On your paper, write the words in parentheses that complete the sentences correctly.

1. (Your, You're) puppy is sleeping in (its, it's) new doghouse.
2. (Its, It's) time for the dog's dinner, and (its, it's) dish is gone.
3. (Its, It's) collar is new.
4. (Its, It's) collar sparkles, and (its, it's) leather.
5. After (your, you're) walk, put (its, it's) leash away.
6. (There, They're) goes (your, you're) airplane.
7. (Its, It's) a new plane.
8. (Its, It's) cockpit is full of gadgets.
9. Now (its, it's) landing near (its, it's) hangar.
10. (Your, You're) the lucky owner of the plane.
11. (There, They're, Their) sits (your, you're) surprise.
12. (Its, It's) in a big red box.
13. Inside, (there, they're, their) are noisy sounds.
14. People listen. (There, Their, They're) surprised by (its, it's) loud sounds.
15. (Your, You're) careful when you lift (its, it's) lid.

Activity C Find the sentences with mistakes in word usage. Write the sentences correctly on your paper. If a sentence is correct, write *C*.

1. Rob and Lena put they're books over their on the shelf.
2. The dog is taking it's time with you're newspaper.
3. Wait your turn, please.
4. Your too late for dinner, but its not too late for dessert.
5. The look on there faces was one of shock.

People often misuse the verbs *lie* and *lay, sit* and *set*, and *rise* and *raise.* To avoid confusion with these verbs, it is important to know the meaning of each word.

Word	Meaning
lie	"to recline" or "to be in a resting position"
lay	"to put" or "to place something"
sit	"to put oneself in a sitting position"(as on a chair)
set	"to place something down"
rise	"to get up" or "to go up"
raise	"to make something go up"

To use these verbs correctly, it is also helpful to know the parts of each verb.

Present	Past	With Helpers
lie	lay	(is) lying, (has) lain
lay	laid	(is) laying, (has) laid
sit	sat	(is) sitting, (has) sat
set	set	(is) setting, (has) set
rise	rose	(is) rising, (has) risen
raise	raised	(is) raising, (has) raised

Finally, it helps to know that *lay, set,* and *raise* may each take a direct object. *Lie* and *rise* never take an object. *Sit* almost never takes an object.

EXAMPLE

No direct object   The lion lay in front of the lake.
Direct object   The lion laid his tail on the ground.
(The lion was in a resting position in front of the lake. The lion placed his tail on the ground. *Tail* is the direct object of *laid.*)

No direct object   Marisa is sitting on the chair.
Direct object   Joaquin set the pen on the desk.
(Marisa is in an upright position on the chair. Joaquin put the pen on the desk. *Pen* is the direct object of *set*.)

No direct object   Adah rarely has risen before ten.
Direct object   Kalifa and Armando have raised the price.
(Adah has rarely gotten up before ten. Kalifa and Armando have made the price go up. *Price* is the direct object of *have raised*.)

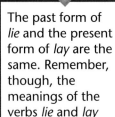

The past form of *lie* and the present form of *lay* are the same. Remember, though, the meanings of the verbs *lie* and *lay* are not the same.

Activity A On your paper, write the verb that completes each sentence correctly. Write the direct object if there is one.

1. The sick child had (lain, laid) in bed for weeks.

2. Her nurse (lay, laid) medicine beside the bed.

3. Her cats are (lying, laying) beside the bed.

4. Books (lay, laid) on the floor all over the room.

5. She will (lie, lay) the papers on the table.

Activity B On your paper, write the verb that completes each sentence correctly. Write the direct object if there is one.

1. Enrique had been (sitting, setting) at the head of the table.

2. Together, the men have (sat, set) a plan on paper.

3. The four men (sit, set) around the table and talk.

4. After the meeting, they (sit, set) business aside.

5. They (set, sat) outside, and watched the sun (set, sit).

Activity C On your paper, write the verb that completes each sentence correctly. Write the direct object if there is one.

1. The sun will (rise, raise) in another hour.

2. Joaquin has always (risen, raised) before dawn.

3. He will (rise, raise) the flag at the courthouse.

4. Soon the temperature will (rise, raise) to 100 degrees.

5. His boss will (rise, raise) his hourly pay.

People often confuse *to, too,* and *two.* These words sound alike but mean different things. *To* is a preposition. *Too* is an adverb that means "also" or "too much." *Two* is a number word that can be an adjective or a noun.

> **EXAMPLE**
>
> | | |
> |---|---|
> | **Preposition** | Sitara and I went to the mall. |
> | **Adverb** | We were too late for the big sale. |
> | **Adjective** | Luckily, there were two sales. |
> | **Noun** | The two of us enjoyed shopping. |

Activity A On your paper, write the word in parentheses that completes each sentence correctly.

1. The stores on Tenth Avenue close (to, too, two) early.

2. Amanda's bike has seats for (to, too, two).

3. Andy's store moved from Fourth Street (to, too, two) Third Avenue.

4. Pete's company moved (to, too, two).

5. My (to, too, two) best friends are Anita and Connie.

People often confuse the verbs *let* and *leave. Let* means "to allow." *Leave* means "to go away." *Leave* can also mean "to stop" or "to let something stay as it is."

> **EXAMPLE**
>
> Let me into the house. (Allow me into the house.)
> Halim will leave the house. (Halim will go away from the house.)
> Leave the gate closed. (Let the gate stay in that position.)

Activity B On your paper, write the word in parentheses that completes each sentence correctly.

1. (Leave, Let) Juanita go to the bus station.
2. The bus will (leave, let) early tonight.
3. Kathy didn't (leave, let) the dog out of the house.
4. Both men (leave, let) the office late on Mondays.
5. The small window doesn't (leave, let) the breeze into the office.
6. (Let, Leave) the dog out now for his walk.
7. Bruce always (lets, leaves) food on his plate.
8. (Let, Leave) me work in peace!
9. (Let, Leave) the window open.
10. You should not (let, leave) anyone disturb you.

Activity C On your paper, write the words in parentheses that complete the sentences correctly.

1. (Let, Leave) the light on so I can see (to, too, two).
2. (To, Too, Two) more names have been added (to, too, two) this list.
3. Don't (let, leave) those animals escape from their cages!
4. Anna (let, leave) the airplane engine warm up.
5. (To, Too, Two) many drivers (let, leave) home at seven o'clock.
6. (Let, Leave) Laura go to the hockey game (to, too, two).
7. (Let, Leave) the cat and the monkey come into the house (to, too, two).
8. (Let, Leave) him alone so he can study.
9. Lightning struck Mr. Smith's house (to, too, two) times.
10. (To, Too, Two) many people tried to (let, leave) through the (to, too, two) doors.

The adverb *too* means "also" when it appears at the end of a sentence. A comma usually comes before *too* in that position.

Example
The stores on the next street close early, *too*.

Double negative

The mistake of using two words that mean "no" in one sentence

You have learned about negatives—words that say *no*. Never use two negatives in the same sentence. A **double negative** is two negatives in one sentence. Double negatives are always incorrect.

Incorrect	I am not never going there.
Correct	I am not going there.
Correct	I am not ever going there.
Correct	I am never going there.

Communication Connection

Using a double negative is always wrong in English. In some languages, however, a double negative calls attention to a negative idea. Think about how you call attention to ideas, negative or positive. In e-mail, for example, capital letters make a word or phrase stand out.

Here is a list of common negative words. Remember that one negative word in a sentence is enough.

hardly	nobody	not	nowhere
never	none	nothing	scarcely
no	no one		

Not often forms part of a contraction. Do not use another negative word in a sentence that has a *not (n't)* contraction.

EXAMPLE

Incorrect	We don't hardly see Paulita anymore.
Correct	We don't see Paulita much anymore.
Correct	We hardly see Paulita anymore.

Here is a list of contractions with *not (n't)*.

aren't	don't	wasn't
can't	hasn't	weren't
couldn't	haven't	won't
didn't	isn't	wouldn't
doesn't	shouldn't	

Activity A Each of these sentences has two or more negative words. Write each sentence correctly on your paper. There may be more than one way to correct each sentence. Write only one correct sentence for each item.

Example	**Incorrect**	We couldn't see hardly nothing in the dark room.
	Correct	We couldn't see anything in the dark room.
	Correct	We could see nothing in the dark room.
	Correct	We could hardly see anything in the dark room.

1. Carlos and Amy didn't see nobody on the street.

2. It don't have no power for hills.

3. The brakes doesn't work no more.

4. She will not buy no more old cars.

5. Mr. Burton won't never live in an old apartment again.

6. His heater don't give no heat.

7. His neighbor never gives him no peace.

8. The owner can't afford no repairs.

9. The owner won't tell Mr. Burton nothing.

10. Mr. Burton won't pay no more money out of his pocket for rent.

Negatives do not travel in pairs.

Writing Tip

When writing about contrasts, use words and phrases such as *however* and *on the other hand* to make your point clear.

Example

The pace of baseball is easy to follow. *However,* the fast action of football is more exciting.

Writers use contrasting words and ideas to help readers understand the differences between two or more things or ideas. For example, you might enjoy one school activity but dislike another. You could contrast the positive points of the activity you like to the negative points of the activity you dislike. On the other hand, you might enjoy both activities but for different reasons. Then you would contrast the reasons each activity appeals to you.

The following is a review of the four steps of the writing process. The example is a contrast between two sports—baseball and football.

1. **Prewrite** The first thing you do before writing is decide what you want to write about. Gather your thoughts and arrange them so that your ideas are easy to understand.

   EXAMPLE   **baseball?**   **football?**
             slow pace   fast action
             easy to follow

2. **Write** Put your thoughts on paper. Write as quickly as you can. Don't worry about mistakes. Just write the ideas. You can correct mistakes later.

   EXAMPLE   Which do I like to watch the best? Football or baseball? Baseball is slow. Football has lots of action. I like both. One is easy to follow. I like both sports.

3. **Rewrite** You want your writing to express your meaning. Go back and read what you wrote. How can you improve it? Rewrite sentences that are unclear.

   EXAMPLE   I like both football and baseball, Its hard for me to decide which one I like best Footbal has more action but baseball is easiest to follow

4. **Edit** Now read your work and correct any mistakes you find. Be sure to check for correct spelling and clear sentences.

> **EXAMPLE** I like both football and baseball. It's hard to decide which one I like better. Football has more action, but baseball is easier to follow.

Activity A Use the writing process to compare cars. Think about two kinds of cars. Which car do you like better? Why do you like it better? Rewrite and edit your comparison to make it better and easier to understand.

Activity B Use the writing process to write a short story about where you would like to live—on a farm, in a city, or in a small town. Which place would make you the happiest? Why is that place best for you? Describe the features of the place that make it better than the others. Write ideas as they come to you. Then rewrite and edit your short story.

Activity C Use the writing process to write a short story about the kind of movies you like. Think about comedies, action movies, horror movies, or science fiction. Which do you enjoy most? Why do you think that type of movie is the best? Write ideas as you think of them. Then rewrite and edit.

Activity D Use the writing process to describe an actor on TV or in the movies. Think about the person and the kinds of things he or she says and does. What does the actor do that you like? Why? What does he or she do that you don't like? Do your friends like the same actor? Why, or why not? Write ideas as quickly as they come to you. Then rewrite and edit.

Abbreviation

Short form of a word

Colon (:)

A punctuation mark used in time

You can write about time in several ways. Days of the week and months of the year begin with capital letters. Seasons do not begin with capital letters. The days of the week and some months of the year have **abbreviations.** An abbreviation is a short form of a word. You should never use abbreviations for the days and the months when writing sentences.

One way to write the time of day is with a **colon (:).** A colon is a punctuation mark that separates the hour from the minutes in time.

> **EXAMPLE**
>
> | | |
> |---|---|
> | **Time** | It's 5:00 A.M. It's 5 o'clock. It's five o'clock. |
> | **Days** | Tuesday, Wednesday, Thursday |
> | **Dates and Special Days** | April 1 is April Fool's Day. |
> | **Seasons** | spring, summer, autumn, winter |
> | **Date** | Saturday, July 5, 2005 |

Activity A On your paper, write these sentences correctly. Put in the missing punctuation marks and capital letters.

1. his flight left on saturday at 730 AM

2. it arrived in texas at 403 PM

3. the last flight left at 4 oclock

4. james made the trip last summer on july 15

5. the 1005 AM train is running late

Activity B Write the full word for each abbreviation.

1. Sun.	**5.** Thurs.	**9.** Feb.	**13.** Sept.
2. Mon.	**6.** Fri.	**10.** Mar.	**14.** Oct.
3. Tues.	**7.** Sat.	**11.** Apr.	**15.** Nov.
4. Wed.	**8.** Jan.	**12.** Aug.	**16.** Dec.

Tuesday

Wednesday

Thursday

Spring

Summer

Winter

Activity C Write each sentence correctly. Change abbreviations to the complete word. Add missing punctuation marks and capital letters.

1. joe set his alarm for 8 oclock on june 1 2005

2. it rang on time every mon. through fri. that summer

3. on nov. 12 his clock stopped at 437 AM

4. every fall squirrels gather nuts in oct. and nov. from the tree outside joes window

5. the noisy animals woke joe at 5 AM one mon.

6. aug. 8 1935 was a thur.

7. my parents flight from rome arrived promptly at 630 PM

8. the theater opens the first fri. in oct.

9. it closes after the winter season on the last tue. in mar.

10. tony made a phone call last wed. at 1130 AM

11. summer school ended on july 28 2006

12. in that state farmers plant crops in late mar. and harvest them in early oct.

13. joan closed the cottage for the winter at noon on sept. 15

14. next wed. the 1115 AM flight to detroit will leave at 2 oclock

15. drama students perform their fall play in nov. and their spring play in apr.

Using What You've Learned

Write a description of your schedule for the coming week. Tell what you will be doing each day. Also tell what time you will be doing it. Include the date with each day. Use capital letters and correct punctuation. Share your schedule with a family member.

Chapter 9 REVIEW

Part A On a sheet of paper, write the correct word or words from the Word Bank to complete sentences 1–3.

1. A _____ is a punctuation mark used in time.

2. Using two words that mean "no" in one sentence is a _____ .

3. An _____ is a short form of a word.

Part B On your paper, write the word in parentheses that completes each sentence correctly.

4. Adam will (accept, except) a job at the laundry.

5. There weren't (no, any) other jobs.

6. (Too, To, Two) many people wanted (too, to, two) work at the laundry.

7. Adam stayed (there, their, they're) until he got the job.

8. (It's, Its) hours are tough, and (it's, its) true that the owners do not pay well; however, (their, they're, there) nice to (their, they're, there) workers.

9. Adam will go (they're, their, there) early in the morning.

10. (Your, You're) going (there, they're, their) with him; don't forget (your, you're) lunch.

11. Please (leave, let) me go to the zoo.

Part C Write the following sentences correctly.

12. the man on the street never saw no pot of flowers

13. our bus stops here at 445 PM every day but sat.

14. I haven't never seen nothing like it

15. tom went to the cabin on sun. dec. 14 2002

16. nobody didn't never mean to hurt him

17. cara finishes work in the summer at 5 oclock

Part D Write notes using important words from each sentence.

18. On Monday, March 24, Frank has an appointment with the dentist at 10:00 A.M.

19. When Anna goes to the grocery store, she needs to buy canned peas, bread, dog food, and a large package of napkins. At the pet store, she needs to buy hamster food.

Part E Use the following notes to write sentences.

20. errands today: grocery store, library, bank

21. meeting 6 P.M.—bring notebook

Part F Write each sentence correctly.

22. after you (sit, set) the table, (sit, set) down near the window

23. a poor test score last sept. (learned, taught) fred a lesson

24. before 1000 AM the temperature inside the house will (rise, raise) 25 degrees

25. (your, you're) remote control (lies, lays) under the sofa

26. last wed. the mail carrier had (laid, lain) a box at the door

Part G

27. Use the writing process to write a short story comparing the most exciting day you can remember to the most boring day you can remember.

Part H On your paper, write the letter of the word that correctly completes each sentence.

28. I don't need _____ help with my chores.

   A no   **B** any   **C** none   **D** not

29. It happened at _____ on Wednesday.

   A 900 PM   **B** 900 P.M.   **C** 9:00 PM   **D** 9:00 P.M.

30. He didn't _____ learn how to whistle.

   A ever   **B** never   **C** not   **D** hardly

Test-Taking Tip   Sometimes it is easier to learn vocabulary words if you break them into their word parts.

10 Making Sentences Work

What makes a winning team? A successful team is a product of teamwork, a process that requires excellent communication. Teammates can communicate in a number of ways. They can convey different kinds of information just through the tone of voice that they choose. Team leaders give instructions, and players ask questions to make sure they understand the shared information.

When we communicate in writing, we cannot "hear" the sound of our teammates' voices. As writers, we must work carefully to make certain that our readers understand the tone in our writing. Since readers cannot ask us verbal questions, we must make sure that our instructions are clear and understandable. On a team, we can communicate through just the sounds of our voices; as writers, we have to depend on word choice, punctuation, and a variety of sentence structures.

In this chapter, you will study how to communicate people's spoken words and feelings in your writing.

Goals for Learning

- ◆ To use punctuation to show tone or mood
- ◆ To write statements, questions, commands, and requests
- ◆ To analyze question pronouns and the structure of question sentences
- ◆ To punctuate direct and indirect quotations correctly
- ◆ To punctuate and capitalize quotations correctly

Tone of voice

The sound of speech

A speaker's words send one message. The **tone of voice,** or sound of the speaker's voice, can reinforce the message or change its meaning. One way to communicate a speaker's tone of voice in writing is through end punctuation.

A sentence that ends in a period makes a statement. The speaker's tone of voice is quiet or neutral. The speaker communicates his or her message mainly through the meaning of the words.

A sentence that ends in an exclamation point shows excitement or strong feeling. The speaker's tone of voice expresses extreme joy, sorrow, horror, surprise, or another strong feeling. An exclamation point tells readers to pay attention. The speaker is saying something that is important to him or her.

A sentence that ends in a question mark asks a question. The speaker's tone of voice is curious. It asks *why, what, how, when,* or *who.* A question mark makes the reader wonder, "What next?"

Notice how different end punctuation changes the meaning and tone of voice of the following sentence.

> **EXAMPLE**   Louisa won the prize.
> (The period shows that the speaker's tone of voice is neutral. The speaker is stating a fact without expressing any particular feeling.)
>
>   Louisa won the prize!
> (The exclamation point shows that the speaker's tone of voice is expressing strong feeling, such as happiness or surprise.)
>
>   Louisa won the prize?
> (The question mark shows that the speaker's tone of voice is expressing curiosity, perhaps even disbelief.)

Activity A On your paper, rewrite each of the following sentences. Add end punctuation marks that express different tones of voice.

1. What is going on here

2. I've told you about this before

3. I won't be going to camp this year

4. Thank you for the beautiful gift

5. What a great gift this is

Interjections can also express tone of voice. Interjections followed by a comma express mild feelings. Interjections followed by an exclamation point show strong feelings.

> **EXAMPLE** Well, look at the time.
> (The comma after the interjection shows that the speaker is mildly concerned about the time.
> Well! Look at the time!
> (The exclamation points show that the speaker is excited or upset about the time.)

Activity B On your paper, rewrite these sentences. Choose punctuation marks that show the tone of voice. Use capital letters after interjections punctuated with an exclamation point.

1. What we have a test today

2. Well I didn't know about it

3. Okay I'll do the best I can

4. Look a new movie is in town

5. Hey it has the biggest stars

Students meet in the hall to discuss the test.

A sentence can make a statement, ask a question, give a command, or make a request.

EXAMPLE

Statement	I can help you.
Question	May I help you?
Command or request	Help me, please.
Strong command or request	Help me, now!

Activity A Follow the directions, and write your own sentences on your paper. Use the examples above to help you.

1. Write a statement using the word *save.*

2. Write a question using the word *save.*

3. Write a command using the word *save.*

4. Write a strong request using the word *stop.*

5. Write a statement using the word *stop.*

We often use the words *can* and *may* in place of each other, but they have different meanings. To use *can* and *may* correctly, remember to:

- Use *can* to show that someone is able to do something.
- Use *may* to show that someone is allowed to do something or to show the possibility that something will happen.

Here is a quick way to remember how to use *can* and *may* correctly. Think of the words *able* and *possible.*

can = able

may = possible

EXAMPLE

Michelle can ride her bicycle now.
(Michelle is able to ride her bicycle now.)

Michelle may ride her bicycle now.
(Michelle has permission to ride her bicycle now, or maybe Michelle will ride her bicycle now.)

Activity B On your paper, use *can* or *may* to write a sentence for each of these ideas.

I am able to:	Maybe I will:
run	go to a store
play games	do my chores
stand	wash my face
read	read
eat dinner	eat dinner

Activity C On your paper, write one question, one statement, one request, and one strong request for each group of words below.

1. John has money problems.

2. Angelina was offered a job.

3. The computer is broken.

4. Susan left for Dallas today.

5. William won a prize on a game show.

Activity D On your paper, write the letter of the correct meaning of each sentence.

> **A** The person is giving a strong command.
>
> **B** The person is able.
>
> **C** The person is giving or asking permission.
>
> **D** The person is making a mild request.

1. She may work at the store.

2. He can work at the store.

3. Get to work now!

4. May I work at the store?

5. I can go to the dance with you.

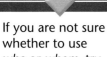

Question pronoun

A pronoun that asks a question

A sentence that asks a question ends with a question mark. Some questions begin with pronouns. A **question pronoun** is a pronoun that forms a question. The pronouns *who, whom, whose, what,* and *which* are question pronouns.

> **EXAMPLE** Who wrote on the table?
> Whose is that?

If you are not sure whether to use *who* or *whom,* try this. Put *he* or *she* where *who* would go. If it sounds right, use *who.*

Other words that form questions include the adverbs *when, where, why,* and *how* and helping verbs such as *will, can, do, have, could, should,* and *would.*

> **EXAMPLE** When will the guests leave?
> Did you see my catch?

When the pronoun *who* begins a question with an action verb, *who* is usually the subject of the sentence. Other question pronouns may also be the subject of action verbs, or they may describe the subject.

> **EXAMPLE** Who wrote on the table?
> What made that sound?
> Which of these cabinets holds the papers?
> Whose glove fell on the ground?

In questions with linking verbs, the subject often follows the verb. The subject of a question may also come between the helping verb and the main verb. Keep in mind that *whom* is an objective case pronoun and can never be the subject of a sentence.

> **EXAMPLE** What is your name?
> Whom did Dad see at the office?
> Why were you so early?
> Are Renaldo and Chad at school?

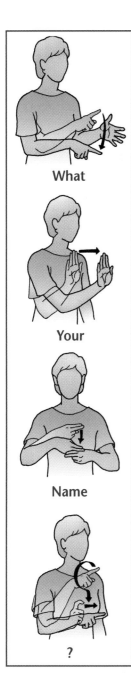

What

Your

Name

?

What is your name?

To find the subject in a question, follow these steps:

1. Find the verb or verb phrase.

2. Ask who or what about the verb.

3. Try to form a statement from the question.

4. Identify the subject.

Activity A Write each question on your paper. Use the above steps to find the subject and verb of each question. Underline the subject. Circle the verb or verb phrase.

1. Did your friends sit near you?

2. Will that stack of books help you with the test?

3. Has Evan parked his car by the pool?

4. Could you bring that book over here?

5. Who runs the old store in town?

6. When does the corner store open?

7. Who bought all that cereal?

8. What will Ilana and Michael find upstairs?

9. Is your class a good one?

10. Are the students in your class friendly?

Activity B Use these words to form questions. Write each question on your paper and underline its subject.

1. who

2. what

3. whose

4. which

5. when

6. where

7. why

8. how

9. will

10. did

Lesson 4 — Compound and Complex Sentences

Complex sentence

A sentence that includes both an independent clause and a dependent clause

Independent clause

A complete sentence

Dependent clause

A group of words that does not form a complete thought and cannot stand alone

You learned in Chapter 3 that a compound sentence has two complete thoughts joined by a conjunction or by a semicolon. Conjunctions such as *and, but,* and *or* join main ideas in a compound sentence.

EXAMPLE

Compound sentence

Alan loves cats, but his cousin is allergic to cat fur.
complete thought   complete thought

A **complex sentence** has an **independent clause** and a **dependent clause.** An independent clause expresses a complete thought and is a sentence. A dependent clause does not express a complete thought. It is not a sentence and cannot stand alone.

EXAMPLE

Complex sentence	Alan works at a radio station on the weekends because he loves music.
Independent clause	Alan works at a radio station on the weekends (a complete thought)
Dependent clause	because he loves music (not a complete thought)

Dependent clause conjunctions join dependent clauses to independent clauses.

Dependent Clause Conjunctions			
after	before	so that	whenever
although	if	unless	where
as	once	until	wherever
because	since	when	while

Compound-complex sentence

A sentence with two or more independent clauses and one or more dependent clauses

Activity A Write each complex sentence on your paper. Underline the independent clause once and the dependent clause twice. Circle the conjunction.

Example Andre's van doesn't work well (since) it is so old.

1. He watches for engine overheating if the hill is steep.

2. His van struggles up the hill while traffic waits.

3. An old van can't climb a steep hill unless it's in good shape.

4. He is surprised whenever his van starts.

5. He will buy a new van when he has more money.

A sentence can be both compound and complex. A **compound-complex sentence** has two or more independent clauses and at least one dependent clause.

> **EXAMPLE**
>
> **Compound-complex sentence**
>
> Alan went home, and I went to the library after school ended.
>
>   two independent clauses   dependent clause

Writing Tip

Few people use compound-complex sentences when they speak. These long sentences are more common in writing. Use them to connect details and make your writing more lively.

Activity B On your paper, write whether each sentence is *compound, complex,* or *compound-complex.*

1. Madalena's grocery cart was full; she shopped for the month.

2. The clerk rang up Madalena's order, which filled twenty bags.

3. We got out of the car, and the dog, which had been asleep on the front porch, sat up and barked.

4. Madalena and I talked while we prepared dinner.

5. Because Madalena bought so much food, the cabinets were full and her whole family was happy.

In some complex sentences, pronouns relate or tie a dependent clause to the rest of the sentence. The pronoun is the subject of the clause.

Pronouns That Begin Dependent Clauses				
that	what	whatever	which	who

EXAMPLE   Brandi, who lives on my block, almost won the match.

A dependent clause can appear at the beginning, in the middle, or at the end of a complex sentence. Use a comma when the dependent clause comes at the beginning or in the middle of the sentence. Do not use a comma when the dependent clause comes at the end of the sentence.

EXAMPLE   Because he was hungry, Nigel went out for lunch.
Nigel, who was hungry, went out for lunch.
Nigel went out for lunch because he was hungry.

Activity A On your paper, write each sentence. Underline the dependent clause. Add commas where needed.

1. Unless his brother goes with him Matthew won't go out.

2. Napoli's Pizza Place which has the best pizza in town is their favorite restaurant.

3. Matthew who loves video games plays and eats at the same time.

4. They stay at Napoli's until their friends arrive.

5. Because it has the best pizza the friends always meet at Napoli's.

Some conjunctions that introduce dependent clauses are also prepositions or part of two-word prepositions. These include *after, before, since, until, as of,* and *because of.*

Do not confuse a prepositional phrase with a dependent clause. A dependent clause has a subject and a verb. A prepositional phrase does not.

EXAMPLE

| **Dependent clause** | We met for dinner after the game ended. |
| **Prepositional phrase** | We met for dinner after the game. |

Activity B On your paper, write whether the underlined words in each sentence are a dependent clause or a prepositional phrase.

1. <u>Before the game,</u> Jon and Sheri studied.

2. <u>Before the game began,</u> Jon and Sheri studied at the library.

3. <u>After the game ended,</u> Jon and Sheri went to the park.

4. <u>After the game,</u> Austin and Dave went to the pool.

5. <u>During the evening,</u> they watched a movie that had captioning.

Communication Connection

Captioning helps people who are hard of hearing enjoy television, films, and videos. Open captioning translates words and sounds into text. The text appears on the screen in a black box.

Complex sentences combine related ideas. Writers use complex sentences to add interest and variety.

EXAMPLE

| **Related ideas** | The baseball season is over. We talked about it. |
| **Complex sentence** | Although the baseball season is over, we talked about it. |

Activity C Combine each pair of sentences to make a complex sentence. Use the dependent clause conjunction in parentheses. Write the sentences on your paper.

1. Athletes can't win. They practice often. (unless)

2. They trained hard. They felt ready. (until)

3. The athletes are heroes. They travel. (wherever)

4. Dave has a new TV set. It has captioning. (because)

5. His mother watches it often. She is hard of hearing. (who)

A **direct quotation** is the exact words that someone says. Use **quotation marks** ("") to enclose the words of a direct quotation. An **indirect quotation** uses other words to tell what someone says. Do not use quotation marks with an indirect quotation.

Direct quotation

The exact words that someone says

Quotation marks ("")

Punctuation used to begin and end a direct quotation

Indirect quotation

What someone says but not his or her exact words

EXAMPLE

Direct quotation   Matt said, "That was a great book!"
Indirect quotation   Matt told Max that the book was great.

Activity A On your paper, write whether the underlined words in each sentence are a *direct quotation* or an *indirect quotation*.

1. Darnay said, "Let's go see a movie."

2. Ray said that he would ask Erica to go.

3. Erica said that she would love to see that movie.

4. "If you pay for the movie, I'll pay for the popcorn," she said.

5. Darnay said, "That's a great idea."

When writing sentences with direct quotations, remember to:

• Capitalize the first word of a direct quotation that is a complete sentence. Always capitalize the first word of a direct quotation that begins a sentence, even if it is not a complete sentence.

• Place a comma right after the words that identify the speaker when the speaker's name comes before the quotation. Place the comma before the final quotation mark when the speaker's name follows the quotation.

• Place the period before the final quotation mark when the quotation ends a sentence that is a statement.

EXAMPLE   Angela said, "Playing volleyball makes me hungry."
"Everything makes you hungry," Max joked.

Activity B On your paper, rewrite the following indirect quotations as direct quotations.

1. Kim said that Candace knows a good play we should see.

2. Candace said that the play will run another month.

3. Andy and Aiesha said that they were going to visit next month.

4. They said that they would like to see the play, too.

5. Candace said that she would like to see the play again.

A direct quotation can be more than one sentence long. Use only one set of quotation marks to enclose the speaker's entire speech.

EXAMPLE   **Angela said,** "The soup was good. Now I want a sandwich."

Activity C On your paper, rewrite the following indirect quotations as direct quotations.

1. Sierra said that she is tired of movies. She prefers TV shows.

2. Madelyn said that she prefers movies. She likes an evening at the theater.

3. Sierra said that it is easier to change channels. She said that she can watch a couple of shows at the same time.

4. Madelyn said that she can't do that. She said that she gets confused.

5. Sierra said that Madelyn should come and spend an evening with her. Sierra said that she would show Madelyn her method of watching two TV shows.

Sierra and Madelyn watch TV together.

It is important to edit your writing carefully. Here are some helpful hints for proofreading your work.

- Look for mistakes in grammar, punctuation, and spelling.
- Check to see that every sentence has a subject and verb and that it expresses a complete thought.
- Make sure that every sentence begins with a capital letter and ends with a punctuation mark.
- Check that the subject and the verb agree. (Singular subjects take singular verbs. Plural subjects take plural verbs.)
- Make sure to use the correct form of a verb to tell about past, present, and future time.

> Proofreading marks show where to make corrections. A caret (^) is a common proofreading mark. It shows where to add a word or punctuation mark.

Activity A On your paper, answer each of the following questions.

1. What are the parts of the writing process?
2. What are the two main parts of a sentence?
3. What are three punctuation marks that end sentences?
4. What are the eight parts of speech?
5. What is the difference between an adjective and an adverb?

Activity B Find and edit the mistakes in each sentence. Write the corrected sentence on your paper.

1. claudio called come and eat dinner
2. after people works hard their hungry
3. claudio a good cook grills thick steaks
4. helen told us that she took a trip to her uncles ranch in texas
5. uncle keshawn and helen talked about there horses while claudio grilled steaks potatoes and fresh corn

When you write, try to include a variety of sentence types. Remember that you can combine ideas in compound, complex, or compound-complex sentences.

Simple
The snow fell. The snow melted. The temperature rose.
Compound
The snow fell, and then it melted; the temperature rose.
Complex
The snow melted as the temperature rose.
Compound-complex
The snow fell and, as the temperature rose, the snow melted.

Activity **C** Combine the ideas in these simple sentences into compound, complex, or compound-complex sentences. Write at least one sentence of each type on your paper.

1. The dog barked. The cat scratched. They fought.

2. The ball bounced. The player jumped. The game ended.

3. Lights dimmed. Music played. The movie started.

4. Monkeys screech. Lions roar. The zoo opens.

5. A rooster crows. A robin sings. A new day dawns.

Activity **D** Use the steps in the writing process to write a short story about Ellen on your paper. Use a variety of sentence types and quotations in your story. Use this information.

Serena asked Ellen to a party. Ellen said she would go. She doesn't know many of the people who will be at the party. Later, her best friend asks her to another party. She talks to her friends about the problem.

1. What do Ellen's friends say? What does Ellen decide to do? What does she tell Serena and her best friend?

2. Rewrite and edit your short story about Ellen.

A direct quotation may stand alone.

EXAMPLE   "The day we quit is the day we lose."

The name of the person quoted can come before, after, or in the middle of the quotation. Notice the placement of the commas that separate the speaker from the quotation in each of these examples.

EXAMPLE

Mr. Hackett said, "The day we quit is the day we lose."
"The day we quit," said Mr. Hackett, "is the day we lose."
"The day we quit is the day we lose," said Mr. Hackett.

If a quotation is a question or an exclamation, place the question mark or exclamation point before the final quotation mark.

EXAMPLE   "Where have you been?" **Kerry asked.**
Susan exclaimed, "What an exciting time we had!"

(Notice that no comma comes before Kerry's name. No end punctuation comes after the quotation marks that enclose an exclamation or a question that ends a sentence.)

Activity A Write these sentences correctly on your paper.

1. Melanie said welcome to my cafe

2. Where is the meal I ordered asked Travis

3. Tom asked quietly zack are you asleep

4. justin's father yelled I thought you were working on the lawn

5. I was working said justin but I took a break

Yell

Ask

Declare

Repeating the verb *said* in sentences can make your writing sound dull. Here is a list of other verbs to use in place of *said* when writing direct quotations.

ask	exclaim	mumble
call out	gasp	whisper
declare	laugh	yell

Activity B Tia is at a ball game. On your paper, write Tia's comments as direct quotations. Try not to repeat the word *said* in your sentences. Look at the list above for words you can use in place of *said*.

Example   Let's play harder
                 Tia yelled, "Let's play harder!"

1. when will this game begin

2. I hope it doesn't rain

3. that was a nice catch

4. don't stop run for third base

5. send in a new pitcher

Activity C Write these compound and complex sentences on your paper. Add capital letters and punctuation.

1. the day was a long one and now i am very tired

2. new york is a nice city but i prefer san diego

3. january is cold june is warm

4. as i sit here i think about my friends and my family

5. when class began mary wasn't there

Using What You've Learned

Write a conversation between yourself and a friend or family member. The conversation can be real or imaginary. Place names of the speakers before, after, or in the middle of quotations. Use a variety of verbs that mean "say." Make sure you have used end punctuation and quotation marks correctly.

Chapter 10 R E V I E W

Word Bank

complex sentence

compound-
complex sentence

dependent clause

direct quotation

independent
clause

indirect quotation

question pronoun

quotation marks

tone of voice

Part A Read each sentence below. Fill in each blank with a vocabulary word that correctly completes each sentence.

1. A group of words that does not form a complete thought and cannot stand alone is a _____ .

2. Place _____ around the words in a direct quotation.

3. A _____ contains both an independent clause and a dependent clause.

4. An _____ uses words other than the speaker's to tell what the speaker says.

5. The sound of a speaker's voice is called _____ .

6. An _____ expresses a complete thought and is a sentence.

7. A pronoun that forms a question is called a _____ .

8. A _____ is the speaker's exact words.

9. A sentence with two or more independent clauses and one or more dependent clauses is a _____ .

Part B Rewrite these sentences, choosing punctuation that shows the tone of voice.

10. Well you should have looked both ways

11. Look there is my math teacher

12. Hey can you go ask him a question

Part C Write one question, one statement, one command, and one strong command for each group of words below.

13. Your neighbor has three dogs

14. I can eat dinner early tonight

15. The computer is fixed.

Part D On your paper, write the subject and the complete verb for each question.

16. Why does Zachary still use that old computer?

17. Has he written good stories on it?

18. Where did Zachary buy it?

19. When will he sell it?

Part E Read each sentence below. Choose the letter next to the word that tells the part of speech of the word in bold.

20. **Which** of the books did you write?

    A question pronoun   **C** adverb

    B verb   **D** subject

21. Why **is** the cat fat?

    A subject   **C** linking verb

    B helping verb   **D** adverb

22. How **can** you learn about the contest?

    A subject   **C** adverb

    B helping verb   **D** linking verb

Part F Write these sentences correctly on your paper. Use punctuation and capital letters.

23. where does the dirt road lead garret asked

24. alice yelled the last movie begins in two minutes

25. you can do it lena exclaimed if you try

Part G Write these sentences on your paper. Underline the independent clause once and the dependent clause twice.

26. The team that won the championship was from Atlanta.

27. Whatever happens, the play will open Saturday.

Part H Write whether each sentence is compound, complex, or compound-complex.

28. When the class bell rang, some students were in the hall.

29. Because the day was hot, Bryan went home early, and Jana went swimming.

30. I am going to the beach, and Tanya is going shopping.

Test-Taking Tip   If you are having trouble solving a problem on a test, go on to the next problem and come back to any skipped problems.

11 Writing for Others

Do you enjoy writing letters? You write letters mainly to communicate with others. How do you make your letters interesting and fun for the people who read them? Do you share important details of your life and the lives of those close to you? Do you include humorous stories about yourself?

A letter is one form of written communication. There are other forms, such as memos, invitations, news articles, directions, stories, and reviews. Whenever you write, your goal is to share information and ideas with readers. To be sure readers understand your ideas, you must present them in a clear, organized way.

In this chapter, you will study different forms of written communication.

Goals for Learning

◆ To write facts in memos, invitations, and news stories

◆ To write paragraphs that describe, that give directions, and that persuade

◆ To write a story, a review, and a letter

Memo

A clear, organized record of important facts and details

Imagine this scene: The phone rings. You answer it. It's for your sister who is out. You take a message, making sure that you write the information clearly and accurately.

People in offices handle situations like this every day. An important part of their jobs is their ability to take and give messages clearly and accurately.

Memo is short for *memorandum.* The word *memorandum* comes from Latin. It means "something that must be remembered." A memo's brief, clear form makes details easy to see and remember.

Many office workers record important messages in **memos.** A memo records facts and details in a clear, organized way. The person reading the memo should not have any questions about the message or its purpose. Look at the example memo below.

EXAMPLE   On January 15 at 2:00 P.M., Mark called. Troy answered the phone. Mark told Troy that it was very important that Kendrell call him back that night before 8:00 P.M. at 945-555-2216.

MEMO

To: Kendrell
From: Troy
Subject: Phone call from Mark
Date: Jan. 15
Time: 2:00 P.M.

He says it is important that you call him back before 8:00 P.M. tonight at 945-555-2216.

Activity A   On your paper, write a memo for each of these phone calls. Use the example as your model.

1. Linda called Joey on December 1 at 3:30 P.M. She wants him to meet her at 5th and State Streets at 5:00 P.M.

2. Peter called for Aaron on January 7 at 7:00 P.M. He wants to borrow one of Aaron's cassette tapes.

3. Kim called on April 2 at 8:00 P.M. She wants Karen to call her tomorrow at work. The number is 766-555-7011.

An **invitation** is a written request. An invitation asks someone to attend a party, a meeting, a lunch, or other event. Like a memo, an invitation presents important information in a clear, organized way. Invitations tell

- what the event is and, usually, its purpose
- when, where, and at what time the event will take place
- who is arranging the event

Most invitations also include a telephone number for an RSVP. This means "please reply" to tell whether you can or cannot attend the event. Often, an invitation gives a date by which to reply. This helps the person planning the event know how many people will attend. Here is an example of an invitation.

You're invited to a celebration!

When:	June 3
What Time:	4:00 P.M.
Where:	1340 Dustpath Way
Given by:	Helen Waite
	To celebrate Tom Waite's graduation
RSVP:	502-555-2072, by May 15

Activity B On your paper, write an invitation to each of these parties.

1. Everett Hull is having a New Year's Eve party on December 31 at 9:00 P.M. at 16 Holland Street. He would like guests to reply by December 20. His phone number is 223-555-7102.

2. Katie Thomas is having a graduation party on June 2 at 2:00 P.M. at 201 South Fourth Street. Her phone number is 678-555-4003.

3. Bill McKay and Jill Johnson just got engaged. Jill's younger sister Amy is having a party for them at 7:00 P.M. on March 4 at 601 West Main. Amy's phone number is 811-555-1767. She wants guests to reply by February 15.

Lead paragraph

A paragraph that introduces a news article; it tells who, what, when, where, why, and sometimes, how

News stories give us facts about current events. We hear news reports on radio and television. We read news articles in newspapers and magazines. The **lead paragraph** in a news article answers the questions *who, what, where, when, why,* and sometimes, *how*.

EXAMPLE

Local Girl Wins Award

Maya Lewis, 1206 Rock Road, won an award at the county festival last Sunday for her giant tomatoes. The tomatoes raised by Lewis were as large as basketballs. When asked how she grew such big tomatoes, Lewis replied, "Water, luck, and my secret plant food."

Who:	Maya Lewis
What:	won an award
Where:	at the county festival
When:	last Sunday
Why:	for her tomatoes
How:	water, luck, secret plant food

Writing Tip

When you write a news story, make the first sentence of your lead paragraph engaging. The first sentence is called the hook. It should catch the reader's attention.

Activity A Read this lead paragraph for a news article. Find the facts that answer the questions below. Write the facts on your paper.

Rivera Wins Sports Honor

Miguel Rivera, 409 Bluewave Blvd., was named "All-State Pitcher" by the State Baseball Association at a conference last Monday. Rivera's fastball helped him pitch five shutouts for the Centerpoint Mustangs last year. The Mustangs finished undefeated.

1. Who?

2. What?

3. Where?

4. When?

5. Why?

6. How?

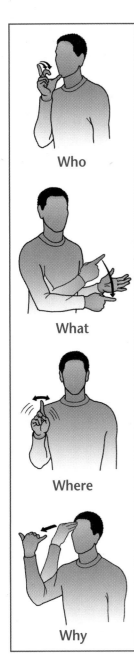

Who

What

Where

Why

The Writing Process

1. **Prewrite** The facts are given for you to use.

2. **Write** Turn the facts into sentences. Write quickly.

3. **Rewrite** Improve your sentences.

4. **Edit** Read your work and correct all mistakes.

Activity B Use the steps above to write a lead paragraph for an article about the events outlined below.

1. *Who:* Joshua Hirsch
What: arrived from Israel
When: Tuesday
Where: New York City
Why: to see a brother he hasn't seen in fifty years

2. *Who:* Enzo Santos
What: won Dry Gulch Auto Race
When: Saturday
Where: Reno, Nevada
Why: best time for the track
How: fastest car and best pit crew

3. *Who:* Elisa Harper
What: slept on her roof
When: Thursday night
Why: to escape floodwaters when dam broke
How: "I climbed out the attic window and onto the roof."

4. *Who:* Ella Schmidt
What: won music contest
When: Friday
Where: Park College
Why: played guitar and drums
How: played original songs and well-known favorites

5. *Who:* Florita Wilson
What: caught a 20-pound catfish
When: Thursday evening
Where: Black Lagoon, Memphis
Why: to win contest for biggest fish
How: used old-fashioned bait—ordinary earthworms

Paragraph

A group of sentences about one topic

Topic

The main idea of an essay or paragraph

Topic sentence

A sentence that states the main idea of a paragraph

Descriptive paragraph

A paragraph that describes a person, place, or thing

A **paragraph** is a group of sentences that tells about one **topic,** or main idea. The **topic sentence** states the main idea of the paragraph. The other sentences in the paragraph relate to, or support, the main idea.

A **descriptive paragraph** describes a person, place, or thing. Use the steps of the writing process to write a descriptive paragraph.

1. **Prewrite** Think about a topic. Write it down. List facts about your topic, along with some descriptive adjectives.

2. **Write** Write a topic sentence. Then write a sentence for each fact on your list.

3. **Rewrite** Improve the paragraph. Combine short sentences into longer ones. Check to see that all the sentences are about the topic. Change the order of sentences if you wish.

4. **Edit** Check your spelling, punctuation, and word use. Make changes for your final copy.

EXAMPLE

Topic sentence
The hillside was beautiful that June morning.
Facts
1. big trees in the field
2. summer wind
3. flowers in the field
4. puffy, white clouds
5. clear, blue sky

Edited Paragraph
    The hillside was beautiful that June morning. A summer wind warmed us. We watched the flowers in the field swaying under puffy, white clouds. Everything glistened under a clear blue sky.

Activity A Use the steps in the writing process to write a paragraph that describes your favorite place. Write your paragraph on your paper.

Writing Tip

To write a
paragraph, you
will probably need
at least three
facts. If you do
not have enough
facts, choose a
different topic.

Activity B Write a paragraph about Gregory Ramos. Use the following topic sentence and supporting facts and details:

Topic sentence
Gregory Ramos was a well-liked person.

Facts and details

1. friendly
2. polite
3. good listener
4. helpful
5. sense of humor
6. honest

Activity C Write a paragraph that describes your dream house. What does it look like? What special features does it have? Be as creative as you wish. Use the steps in the writing process to write your paragraph.

Activity D Write a paragraph about a special moment in time. Use the steps in the writing process as you create a descriptive paragraph with the following information:

Topic sentence
The senator from Ohio spoke to the class.

Facts and details

1. on the lawn in front of school
2. students gathered
3. principal introduced senator
4. senator talked
5. people asked questions
6. warm afternoon in April

Activity E Write a paragraph about the best or most important moment in your life. Use the steps in the writing process to write your paragraph.

Students gather to listen to a speech.

Process paragraph

A paragraph that tells how to do something

You can write a paragraph to explain how to do something. A **process paragraph** explains step-by-step how to do something. When you are writing a process paragraph, it is important to include each step of the process and to order the steps in the correct sequence.

1. **Prewrite** Think about a topic sentence. Write it down. Add a list of steps.

2. **Write** Write a sentence for each step on your list. Keep your sentences about the steps short and easy to follow.

3. **Rewrite** Improve the paragraph. Check to see that you have not left out any steps. Be sure your sentences are in the right order.

4. **Edit** Check your spelling, punctuation, and word use. Make changes for your final copy.

Words that tell the order of steps are important. Help readers follow your order by using words such as *first, second, third, next, last, then, before,* and *after.*

EXAMPLE

Topic sentence
Bowling can be fun when you relax and follow these simple directions.
Steps
1. Hold the ball in front of you.
2. Take three steps toward the pins.
3. Roll the ball down the alley on your last step.
Edited paragraph
    Bowling can be fun when you relax and follow a few simple directions. First, hold the ball in front of you. Next, take three steps toward the pins. Finally, roll the ball down the alley on your last step.

Activity A Write a process paragraph about sharpening a pencil. Watch someone sharpen a pencil. List each step. Then follow the rest of the writing process to complete your paragraph.

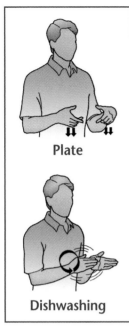

Plate

Dishwashing

Washing the dishes

Activity B The steps in the following process paragraph are out of order. Put the steps in the correct order. Then rewrite the paragraph correctly on your paper.

Changing a Lightbulb

● The lightbulb in the table lamp has burned out, and the lamp needs a new bulb. Twist the new lightbulb into the socket. Remove the lamp shade. Take the old lightbulb out of the socket by twisting the bulb counterclockwise, or starting toward the left. Put the lamp shade back on the lamp. Unplug the lamp from the wall. Plug the lamp into the wall outlet ● again. Now the lamp is fixed.

Riding a bicycle

Activity C Choose three of the following topics. On your paper, write a process paragraph about each topic. Be sure to follow the steps in the writing process.

Riding a Bicycle	Playing a Video Game
Making a Sandwich	Fixing a Flat Tire
Selecting a Library Book	Making Cookies
Dialing Long Distance	Setting an Alarm Clock
Washing the Dishes	Wrapping a Present
Planting a Tree	Playing a Sport
Ironing a Shirt	Playing a Musical Instrument
Walking on Ice	Shopping for Shoes
Waxing a Car	Making Breakfast
Mowing the Lawn	Planning a Party

Persuasive paragraph

A paragraph that tries to make readers believe something or do something

Have you ever made up your mind to do something or believe something because you're sure that you are right? Then, you may have read something that persuaded you to change your mind. A **persuasive paragraph** tries to convince readers to think or act a certain way. When you write a persuasive paragraph, include language that will make people think and feel as you do.

1. **Prewrite** Write down something you would like to persuade others to do. List reasons why others should believe the way you do about this topic.

2. **Write** Write a topic sentence that states your purpose (to persuade readers to do something). Then write sentences for each reason you listed.

3. **Rewrite** Check to see that you have listed all the reasons you can think of to support your topic. Change or add words that will make your paragraph more persuasive.

4. **Edit** Check your spelling, punctuation, and word use. Make changes for your final copy.

EXAMPLE   Justin's manager has decided to lay him off to cut costs at work. Justin must persuade his manager not to lay him off.

Topic sentence
I am a good employee for this company.

Facts
1. finish tasks quickly
2. arrive early
3. work after hours sometimes
4. skills worth my wage

Edited paragraph
    I am a good employee for this company. I believe my skills are worth the wage I receive. I always arrive at work early; often, I work after hours. I complete my tasks quickly. I believe I should continue working here.

Activity A On your paper, write a persuasive paragraph about why your friends should study with you tonight. Use the steps of the writing process to write your paragraph. Here are some possible reasons you might use to support the topic that you and your friends should study together. You can add reasons of your own.

- There is a test tomorrow.
- We can share ideas.
- We can read one another's notes.
- We can practice saying facts out loud.
- We can correct one another's work.

Here is a possible topic sentence:

Our group of friends should study together.

Activity B Rewrite and edit this persuasive paragraph to improve it. You may change the order of the sentences. You may combine sentences, and you may write additional sentences.

My dog Monty is not dangerous. He has never bittes. He doesn't growls at strangers. He a friendly dog Monty likes peple. When he jumps up on other's he's just saying helo. I keep Monty on a leash. When we walk But, it's not because he's a mean dog. very nice Every one likes Monty.

Activity C Choose two of these topics. Write a persuasive paragraph for each one.

1. Your favorite sports team is the best.

2. People should vote in elections.

3. Your town (or city or state) has more to offer than other places in the country.

4. Being a child (or teenager, young adult, or senior citizen) is better than being in any other age group.

5. Regular exercise is important for good health.

Narrative
———
A series of paragraphs that go together to tell a story

A **narrative** is a series of paragraphs that tell what happens in a story. Notice how each paragraph in the following narrative helps tell the story.

EXAMPLE   **Jerod's Balancing Trick**

1   Jerod and his friend Cordell went to a carnival. A woman in a costume walked on a rope high above the ground. Jerod thought this trick looked easy.

2   The next day, Jerod stretched a rope in the air between two trees in his yard. "Anybody can do this," Jerod said.

3   "That trick is not easy," replied Cordell.

4   Jerod grabbed a pole and walked proudly to the rope. He put one foot on the rope, then the other foot. He felt like the woman in the show.

5   "Go, go!" Cordell yelled. He waved his arms and grinned.

6   Jerod's legs shook. The rope shook. Jerod shook. His legs wobbled trying to keep straight. He dropped the pole and fell on the grass.

7   Later, Jerod said, "You were right, Cordell. This trick is for experts. It's scary business. I'm still shaking!"

8   Cordell laughed. "Your balancing trick was only two feet off the grass!" he said.

Activity A   Write the answer to each question about the example narrative.

1. Which paragraph introduces the story characters? What are the characters' names?

2. Where does most of the story take place? Which paragraph tells you this?

3. What does Jerod want to do? What does Cordell say to try to get Jerod to change his mind?

4. Which paragraphs have descriptive details only and no words spoken by the characters?

5. Why does Cordell laugh at the end?

Dialogue

Conversation between two or more characters in a story

One way writers make a story interesting is by using **dialogue.** Dialogue is conversation between two or more characters. Dialogue helps readers know what the characters are like and why they act the way they do. A new paragraph begins each time the speaker changes or the topic changes.

Another way writers make a story interesting is by adding a twist at the end that surprises or shocks readers.

Activity B On your paper, list ways that the writer made "Jerod's Balancing Trick" interesting for you.

Activity C Write the following as a story. Remember to begin a new paragraph each time the speaker changes.

"Hi," said Valerie. "Well, hello," said Maurice. "It's nice to see you again," said Valerie. "Thanks," said Maurice. "I'm heading for the mall," said Valerie. "Me, too," said Maurice. "I'll go with you, but let's stop for lunch before we go." "Great idea! I'm hungry," said Valerie. "Maybe we could go to the theater later." Then Maurice said, "Maybe we should skip the mall and catch a movie."

Every story has a beginning, a middle, and an ending. The beginning introduces the setting, the characters, and the main character's goal. The middle tells how the main character tries to achieve the goal. The ending tells what happens when the main character reaches the goal.

Everyone knows that characters are a basic element, or part, of a story. Setting is another basic story element. Setting is *where* and *when* a story takes place.

Activity D Here is the beginning of a story. Use the writing process to write a middle and an ending. Be creative.

The Fortune Hunter

Each day at 8:00 A.M., Olindo is at the river. He dips his bucket into the cold, swirling water. Slowly, he pours mud and rocks from his bucket. His hands search for bits of treasure. Time passes, and the heat drains his strength.

One afternoon . . .

What happens to Olindo? What does he do? Are any other people involved?

Review

A writer's opinion about a movie, TV show, book, or play

Have you recently seen a movie that you really liked? Perhaps you saw a TV program that you disliked. You can write your ideas about a movie or a television program as a **review.** A review tells one person's opinion about a movie, TV program, play, or written work.

1. **Prewrite** Think about something you read or saw recently. Write it down. Did you like it or not? List your reasons for liking or disliking this work.

2. **Write** Write a topic sentence that states your opinion. Write a sentence for each supporting reason on your list.

3. **Rewrite** Improve the paragraph as you rewrite it.

4. **Edit** Correct your spelling, punctuation, and word use.

EXAMPLE   **Topic sentences stating different opinions**
1. This movie was fun and entertaining.
2. This movie didn't have a point.

Reasons

First opinion	Second opinion
real characters	no plot
good jokes	bad acting
lively music	boring

Edited paragraphs
1. This movie was fun and entertaining. It had characters who seemed real. They told some good jokes. I also thought the music was lively and original.
2. This movie didn't have a point. It had no plot. The actors spoke with no expression, and the movie was boring.

Activity A Read the story below. Then, on your paper, write a review of the story. State your opinion clearly. Give at least three reasons for your opinion.

> When Carl was eight years old, he got trapped in an old well. Carl and his cousin Simon were playing in a field on the family farm. They spotted the old well and went over to look at it. Simon dared Carl to go down into the well. Carl climbed down into the well. He went about six feet down and stood on a ledge inside the well. Simon looked down at him and waved. Carl waved back. Suddenly, the ledge crumbled beneath Carl and he fell down deeper into the well. Carl and Simon both screamed with fear! Carl's father, Edward, heard the screams and came running over to Simon. Simon told him that Carl had fallen down in the well. Edward looked down into the well and called to Carl. Carl yelled back to his father. He had fallen about six more feet down. Edward ran to the barn and got a ladder. He quickly returned and lowered the ladder into the well. Carl climbed up the ladder and jumped into his father's arms. He had suffered some bumps and bruises when he fell, but otherwise he was all right. Carl and Simon decided never to dare each other again.

Communication Connection

People use body language to show their opinion of a live performance, such as a play or concert. If you like a performance, when it is over you can clap your hands. If you really love it, you can stand up and clap your hands. This is called a standing ovation.

Activity B Write a review paragraph for one of these events.

1. a concert

2. a TV show

3. a club activity

4. a sports activity

5. a play

Activity C Write a review about one of these topics.

1. a book you have read

2. a movie or TV show you have seen

3. a song you have sung or heard

4. a favorite activity of your friends

5. a computer game you have played

Heading

The address of the person writing the letter

Greeting

Word or phrase used before the name or title of the person to whom a letter is sent

Body

The message part of a letter

Closing

Word or phrase used before the signature in a letter

Signature

The name signed by the writer of the letter

You write friendly letters to people you know. Friendly letters share news about yourself and let people know you care about them.

Friendly letters follow a form that includes a **heading,** a **greeting,** a **body,** a **closing,** and a **signature.** The heading gives the address of the writer; the date follows it. The greeting addresses the person receiving the letter. *Dear Mary* is an example of a greeting. The body of the letter contains the message. The closing is a polite word or phrase that ends the letter. The signature is the name of the person writing the letter.

Heading _____
_____

Date _____

Greeting _____ ,
Body _____
_____
_____
_____
_____
_____
_____
_____
_____
_____

Closing _____ ,
Signature _____

Read the letter on the next page from Melinda to her friend Larissa.

36 Plains Avenue
Minneapolis, Minnesota
55406
January 17, 2004

Dear Larissa,

It's always nice to get a message from you. I enjoy hearing about your town. Your new neighbors sound like nice friends.

Your old classmates here miss you. We often wish that you were here. We missed your help at the party last month. You think of funny games.

The school is planning a trip to Williamsburg next year. Everybody is excited. We earned some money from book sales and painting. I hope you and I can meet when we are there. I'll write again when I have more ideas, and we can plan.

Everyone is hoping you'll come for a week next year. We'd love to have you stay with us.

Sincerely,
Melinda

Activity A On your paper, answer the following questions about Melinda's letter.

1. What is Melinda's address? Why is her address in the letter?
2. When did Melinda write the letter?
3. What greeting does Melinda use? What end punctuation mark follows the greeting?
4. What closing does Melinda use? What end punctuation mark follows the closing?
5. How does Melinda let Larissa know that she cares about her?

Using What You've Learned

Write a friendly letter to someone you have not seen for a while. Tell him or her what you have been doing lately. Use the correct form for a friendly letter.

It is important to address an envelope correctly. This will ensure that your letter reaches the person to whom you are writing.

Put two addresses on the outside of an envelope. Print your return address in the upper left-hand corner. Print the address of the person to whom you are writing in the center of the envelope. The person's title and name are on the first line. The street address is on the second line. The city, state or province, and ZIP or postal code are on the third line.

Use the short or full form for state or province names. Print clearly or type the entire address on the envelope.

EXAMPLE

MS MELINDA AIELLO
36 Plains Avenue
Minneapolis MN 55406–2023

Name: _____ → MS LARISSA JOHNSON
Street: _____ → 123 WEST MAIN AVENUE
City, State ZIP Code: _____ → RESTON VA 22091–1234

Activity A Write each address as it should appear on an envelope.

1. Dr. John Hall, 708 Center Terrace Drive, Columbus, Ohio 43201–5986

2. Mrs. Ellen Park, 5 Allen Street, Vance, South Carolina 29163–6983

3. Dr. Rita Ponce, 289 Superior Avenue, Winnipeg, Manitoba, Canada R3T 3XI

4. Mr. Marco Perry, 16 Henry Place, Omega, Georgia 31775–3911

5. Ms. Jane Smith, 25 Northfield Avenue, Port Charlotte, Florida 33952–1164

Activity B Match the words with their meanings. Write each number and its correct letter on your paper.

Words	Meanings
1. paragraph	**A** goes in the upper right-hand part of a letter
2. topic sentence	**B** goes just above the signature
3. heading	**C** group of sentences about one topic
4. date	**D** tells the main idea of a paragraph
5. closing	**E** goes under the heading

Activity C Edit the following sentences. Write the edited sentences on your paper.

1. Helenas house hasn't no yard

2. School start in a few week I hope I do good

3. I gets up early when I go to work lorena said

4. Kelly wisht she had wait for her frend on main street

5. too baby lions arrived at the washington zoo arent they cute

6. that music is much too loud shouted tom

7. you're new computer program wont never fit this machine

8. what you doing kerry asked

9. Im writing a letter to me friend in detroit said susan to kerry

10. Susan went to mailing off a letter

Many people keep in touch with friends by writing letters.

Chapter 11 R E V I E W

Part A Match each of the following vocabulary words with its definition.

Words	Definitions
1. body	**A** a conversation between two or more characters
2. closing	
3. descriptive paragraph	**B** a record of important facts or details
	C a sentence that states the main idea
4. dialogue	**D** a group of sentences about one topic
5. greeting	**E** the words before the signature in a letter
6. heading	**F** a series of paragraphs that tell a story
7. invitation	**G** the main idea of a paragraph or essay
8. lead paragraph	**H** a paragraph that tells how to do something
9. memo	**I** a paragraph that describes someone or something
10. narrative	
11. paragraph	**J** the address of the person writing a letter
12. persuasive paragraph	**K** the words before the name of the person who receives a letter
13. process paragraph	**L** a paragraph that introduces a news article
	M the message part of a letter
14. review	**N** a paragraph that tries to make readers believe or do something
15. signature	
16. topic	**O** the signed name of the writer of a letter
17. topic sentence	**P** a writer's opinion about something
	Q a written request

Part B

18. Imagine that you fell asleep today and woke up in twenty years. Write a five-sentence paragraph to describe the things you might see.

Part C On your paper, write these sentences as a conversation between Jordan and Arisa.

19. hello jordan said arisa hi arisa said jordan arisa said i am moving to kansas city missouri i will miss you said jordan we will still be friends arisa said

Part D Write the answers for each item on your paper.

20. List the facts you need for a party invitation.

21. List the facts you need for a news story.

Part E

22. Write a memo for this phone call. Include these things: To whom, From whom, Subject, Date, Time, and Message.

Saul called on October 15 at 5:15 P.M. He wants Ramone to call him about the time and place of the tennis game.

Part F Choose the letter that correctly answers each question.

23. A pretend person who appears in a story is a _____ .

    A writer   **B** fact   **C** character   **D** hero

24. All appear on an envelope EXCEPT _____ .

    A the writer's telephone number

    B the ZIP or postal code

    C the return address

    D the title of the person who will receive the letter

25. The words "Love, Yasmine" in a letter are _____ .

    A a closing and a signature   **C** a closing

    B a greeting   **D** a heading

Test-Taking Tip When a test question asks you to write a paragraph, make a plan first. Write the main idea for your paragraph. List the supporting details you can include. Then write the paragraph.

12 Spelling

Y ou probably recognize the two small animals shown in the picture. But do you know how to spell this animal's name? Is it "deer," or is it "dear"? One of these words is a noun that names a four-legged mammal, and one is an adjective used to show affection.

Correct spelling can be a challenge. Many English words, such as *deer* and *dear* or *brake* and *break,* have the same sounds but different spellings. Other words, such as "though" or "rough," are not spelled the way they sound. In addition, many words have irregular plural forms and do not end in *-s* or *-es.* For example, you see two animals in the illustration but you would not say, "I see two deers." Since "deer" is a plural word as well as a singular one, the proper usage is "I see two deer."

Certain rules will help you spell most English words correctly. However, you may have to memorize some spellings that are exceptions to these rules.

In this chapter, you will study ways to help you spell better.

Goals for Learning

◆ To practice spelling common problem words

◆ To choose the correct spelling of words that sound alike

◆ To learn rules for forming plurals

◆ To practice spellings of word endings

◆ To learn rules for words that use *ie* and *ei*

It can be easier to spell some words if you break them into smaller parts. Learn to spell the word part by part. Try spelling the word *accident* this way: *ac-ci-dent*.

The more you practice a skill, the easier that skill becomes. Spelling is a skill that takes practice. Focus your practice on words that give you trouble. Soon you will be able to spell those words with ease.

Here are four steps that you can use to practice spelling a new or difficult word.

1. Copy the word on your paper correctly.

2. Write the word again while you say it aloud.

3. Cover the word. Say it. Then write it as you spell it aloud.

4. Check your spelling. If you have spelled the word incorrectly, return to steps 2 and 3.

People often misspell the following words. You may find that learning their spellings is easier if you study the words in small groups.

Group 1	Group 3	Group 5	Group 7	Group 9
accident	disturb	instead	once	study
arctic	doctor	judge	paid	thought
athletic	February	knock	pleasant	toward
beggar	finally	maybe	pretty	trail
beginning	forgot	minute	probably	trial
boundary	forty	misspell	review	Wednesday

Group 2	Group 4	Group 6	Group 8	
calendar	fourteen	necessary	safety	
children	government	nickel	sentence	
consider	grammar	nineteen	shovel	
curious	guard	ninety	since	
decide	history	occur	speak	
destroy	hundred	often	speech	

Activity A Find the misspelled word in each sentence. Write the word correctly on your paper.

1. The artic cold froze my toes.

2. Alec's car was in an acident, but he had the car fixed.

3. Our school has the best atletic teams in the state.

4. He was once a poor begger; now he's rich and famous.

5. This is the begining of a long movie.

6. The fence marks the boundry of our property.

7. Lots of childern play in the park during the summer.

8. The members of the jury will concider the case in private.

9. I was cureous about the contents of the big box.

10. The results of this test will diside my grade for the term.

Activity B Find the misspelled word in each sentence. Write the word correctly on your paper.

1. The raging fire will destory the forest lands.

2. My mother was quiet so she would not desturb my sleep.

3. Call the docter if your fever gets any higher.

4. Valentine's Day is on Febuary 14.

5. The letter from my best friend finaly arrived.

6. Over fourty people came to the big party.

7. My sister will be forteen years old next May.

8. Members of goverment meet in the capitol building.

9. Sue earns high grades on her grammer tests.

10. Adam is in trouble; he fourgot his homework.

Remember that a capitol building is spelled with an o.

Homonym

A word that sounds like another word but has a different meaning and spelling

Homonyms are words that sound alike but have different meanings and different spellings. You can figure out which homonym to use by thinking about the meaning of the other words in the sentence.

Writing Tip

Because they sound alike, it is easy to confuse homonyms. The one sure way to use the word with the correct meaning is to learn which meaning goes with which spelling.

EXAMPLE

Homonyms		Definitions
been	(verb)	past form of *be*
bin	(noun)	a box used for storage
blue	(adjective)	a color; feeling sad
blew	(verb)	past form of *blow*
break	(verb)	to destroy
	(noun)	time off
brake	(noun)	used to stop a car, bike, truck, or other vehicle
buy	(verb)	to pay for something
by	(preposition)	beside; near; within a certain time
dear	(adjective)	loved
deer	(noun)	animal
fair	(noun)	a show with amusements
	(adjective)	pleasing; average; just
fare	(noun)	the price of a ride
for	(preposition)	used to show the purpose or a reason
four	(noun)	a number

Activity A Write the homonym in parentheses that completes each sentence correctly.

1. Jon put trash in the (been, bin).

2. She has (been, bin) here before.

3. Jennifer has a new (blue, blew) bike.

4. The wind (blue, blew) hard all night.

5. Kerry feels (blue, blew) because her friend Amahl is moving to Detroit.

6. Be careful, or you will (break, brake) the glass.

7. Put your foot on the (break, brake) right now and stop this car.

8. Juanita was tired, so she took a (break, brake) from studying.

9. The new calf stands (buy, by) its mother.

10. Derek will (buy, by) a new suit for his grandmother's birthday party.

11. His grandmother is a (dear, deer) person; everyone loves her.

12. The (dear, deer) are shy and run back into the woods whenever anyone comes near them.

13. We had (fair, fare) skies today with lots of sunshine.

14. Jill got on the bus and paid her (fair, fare).

15. Sarah won a blue ribbon for her apple pie at the county (fare, fair).

16. Tamra said that she would be back home (buy, by) dinnertime.

17. That toy is very (dear, deer) to the little boy.

18. Do you think these new game rules are (fair, fare)?

19. Max bought (for, four) apples.

20. He wants a hot dog (for, four) lunch.

Activity B Rewrite and edit this paragraph. Correct the spelling, grammar, and punctuation. Try to improve the paragraph by adding words and combining ideas.

> Peg said It isnt fare I by a TV set it doesn't work I didn't brake it It just blue up buy the time I got back to the store it was close i went home and threw my new TV in the trash been. It just isnt fare.

Remember that homonyms are words that sound alike but have different meanings and spellings. Follow these steps to know which homonym to use in a sentence:

1. Think about the meaning of the other words in the sentence.

2. Think about the meaning of the homonyms.

3. Choose the homonym that makes sense in the sentence.

Practice using these homonyms in sentences.

EXAMPLE

Homonyms		Definitions
hear	(verb)	to listen to
here	(adverb)	this place
hoarse	(adjective)	harsh, scratchy
horse	(noun)	an animal
hour	(noun)	60 minutes; time
our	(pronoun)	belonging to us
knew	(verb)	past form of *know;* understood
new	(adjective)	recent; fresh
know	(verb)	to understand
no	(adjective)	not any
plain	(adjective)	not fancy
	(noun)	flat, wide-open land
plane	(noun)	airplane
so	(adverb)	very
	(conjunction)	in order that
sew	(verb)	to stitch cloth with thread
son	(noun)	male child
sun	(noun)	source of heat and light
weather	(noun)	climate
whether	(conjunction)	if (used with *or*)

Activity A Write the homonym in parentheses that completes each sentence correctly.

1. She didn't (hear, here) me call her name.
2. (Hear, Here) is the money I owe you.
3. Anna will ride the black (hoarse, horse) to the ranch.
4. The coach's voice is (hoarse, horse) from yelling.
5. We met (hour, our) parents for dinner.
6. I'll meet you in one (hour, our).
7. I (knew, new) all the answers but one.
8. We moved into a (knew, new) house.
9. She does not (know, no) the answer to the last question.
10. We were late for dinner, and there was (know, no) food left.
11. They rode in a covered wagon across the grassy (plain, plane).
12. A small silver (plain, plane) landed at the airport.
13. Maria wore a (plain, plane) black dress to the party.
14. Tim baby-sat (sew, so) his parents could go out.
15. She will (sew, so) the tear in her pants.
16. I'm (sew, so) sorry you can't come with us to the movies.
17. The (son, sun) will set at 6:30 P.M.
18. Adam is Shelby's (son, sun).
19. He could not decide (weather, whether) he should go home early or stay late.
20. Today's (weather, whether) will be cloudy and warm.

Activity B Rewrite and edit this paragraph. Correct the spelling, grammar, and punctuation. Try to improve the paragraph by adding words and combining ideas.

> it was the midle of the night I new there was something wrong. I could here the sound of a horse voice It was almost an our before I learnt the cause of the problem Hour knew neighbor has for big parrots and they talk to each other. Now that I no, I can sleep

Lesson 4 Plurals—Two or More

Singular
One

Plural
More than one

A **singular** noun names one person, place, or thing. A **plural** noun names more than one person, place, or thing. Add *-s* or *-es* to most singular nouns to form their plurals.

EXAMPLE

Singular	Plural
door	doors
rake	rakes
inch	inches
wish	wishes
dress	dresses

Activity A Write each singular noun on your paper. Next to each noun, write its plural.

1. hat	**6.** school	**11.** box
2. frog	**7.** building	**12.** pass
3. fire	**8.** truck	**13.** watch
4. town	**9.** bike	**14.** bush
5. rock	**10.** road	**15.** bus

To form the plural of most nouns that end in *-y*, change the *y* to *i* and add *-es*. To form the plural of nouns that end in a vowel plus *-y*, add *-s*.

EXAMPLE

Singular	Plural
hobby	hobbies
way	ways

Activity B Write each singular noun on your paper. Next to each noun, write its plural.

1. sky	**6.** library	**11.** guy
2. toy	**7.** daisy	**12.** bakery
3. glossary	**8.** family	**13.** copy
4. fly	**9.** key	**14.** valley
5. lady	**10.** day	**15.** monkey

A dictionary is handy when you cannot remember the plural of a noun. Look up the singular noun. The dictionary often gives the plural spelling if it is unusual.

Add *-s* to some words that end in *-f* or *-fe* to form their plurals. For other words that end in *-f* or *-fe*, change the *f* or *fe* to *v* and add *-es*.

EXAMPLE

Singular	Plural
chief	chiefs
life	lives

Activity C Write each singular noun on your paper. Next to each noun, write its plural.

1. leaf   **6.** half

2. shelf   **7.** yourself

3. calf   **8.** wolf

4. loaf   **9.** elf

5. thief   **10.** wife

Some nouns form their plurals in irregular ways. Some nouns do not change at all to form their plurals.

EXAMPLE

Singular	Plural
child	children
man	men
woman	women
foot	feet
mouse	mice
goose	geese
tooth	teeth
sheep	sheep
deer	deer

Activity D Write each sentence correctly on your paper. Change the singular nouns in bold to plural nouns.

1. The two **man** were diving from **cliff.**

2. Their **tooth** chattered from the cold.

3. Two **mouse** ran across both of her **foot.**

4. Three **child** each paid five **penny** to pet the **sheep.**

5. Both **library** are closed on **Sunday.**

Writing Tip

Never guess about the spelling of a word. Say the word aloud. List some possible spellings. Look for each spelling in the dictionary. Use the correct spelling when you find it.

You can add endings to many words to make new words.

When adding an ending to a word that ends in -*e*, drop the final *e* if the ending starts with a vowel. Do not drop the *e* if the ending starts with a consonant.

EXAMPLE			
love + less	=		loveless
love + ly	=		lovely
love + ing	=		loving
love + able	=		lovable

When adding an ending that begins with a vowel to one-syllable words with a short vowel sound, double the final consonant before adding the ending.

EXAMPLE			
drop + ed	=		dropped
skip + ed	=		skipped
bat + ing	=		batting
plan + ing	=		planning

Some words do not follow the spelling rules. If you are not sure how to spell a word with an ending added, check the dictionary.

EXAMPLE			
awe + ful	=		awful
courage + ous	=		courageous
wax + ing	=		waxing
mile + age	=		mileage

Lovely

Careful

Careless

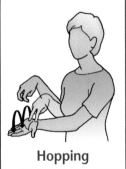

Hopping

Activity A Add the endings to each of the following words. Write the new words on your paper.

1. care + ful
2. care + ing
3. care + less
4. fame + ous
5. flame + less
6. prime + ary
7. safe + ty
8. bride + al
9. like + ly
10. like + ness

Activity B Add the endings to each of the following words. Write the new words on your paper.

1. flag + ed
2. hit + ing
3. hop + ing
4. let + ing
5. step + ed
6. spin + ing
7. slap + ing
8. shop + ed
9. rub + ing
10. win + er

Activity C Rewrite and edit this paragraph. Correct the spelling, grammar, and punctuation. Try to improve the paragraph by adding words and combining ideas.

The bater steped to the plate he is planing on hiting a home run. The pitcher is rubing the ball. the pitcher is the hotest, fasttest player in the league. The ball is spining. The bater carefuly conects with the ball fans in the stands make an aweful noise. The ball skipps across the fence for a home run. It realy is a good game

Words with the vowel pairs *ie* and *ei* often cause spelling problems.

Write *i* before *e* when the vowel sound is long *e* except after the letter *c*.

EXAMPLE	believe	field	receive	deceit
Exceptions	either	seize	weird	

Write *e* before *i* when the vowel sound is not long *e*.

EXAMPLE	weigh	eight	forfeit	neighbor
Exceptions	view	friend	conscience	

In a special notebook, list words that you always have trouble spelling. Then you can review the words from time to time. Before you know it, you will spell the words correctly.

Activity A Add *-ei* or *-ie* to each of the following words. Write the words on your paper.

1. rel_ _f
2. f_ _ld
3. rec_ _ve
4. n_ _ghbor
5. ch_ _f

6. dec_ _ve
7. pr_ _st
8. rec_ _pt
9. gr_ _ve
10. n_ _ce

11. c_ _ling
12. l_ _sure
13. for_ _gn
14. bel_ _f
15. _ _ght

Activity B Find the misspelled words in these sentences. Write the words correctly on your paper. A sentence may have one or more mistakes.

1. Ken plays iether first base or right feild.
2. He has a batting avrage of .300.
3. Tom has been hiting the ball hard latly, to.
4. A fast inside pitch nocked off his glases.
5. The picher through another fastball.
6. Ken told the coachs that he needed some releif as he droped his bat.

7. Woodcrest is one of the busyest towns in the whole state.

8. People try seting new records buy doing some very wierd things.

9. The doctor wrote down Hakim's hight and weight at his yearly physical.

10. Alice went to three scools last year because her famaly moved so offen.

11. The dentist said that Jane's wisdom tooths had to be pulled.

12. Hour nieghbor's dog has ieght of the cutest little puppys you ever saw.

13. I like to play with them in my liesure time.

14. My friend Toshiro peted one of the puppys.

15. Wendy is learning a foriegn language.

16. He recieved the funnyest letter from his neice.

17. Six mouses made a nest behind the stove.

18. The three mans fixed the crack in the cieling.

19. Suri holds strong believes about that topic.

20. I read an aweful reveiw of his lattest play.

Remember to change the y *to an* i *and add* -es *to make the word* puppies.

Writing Tip

Always proofread your writing for spelling errors. Be careful with spell checkers. You may want *loose* but write *lose.* Since *lose* is spelled correctly, the spell checker may not help you.

Some words with similar spelling patterns and similar sounds can cause spelling problems. People often confuse these words. Be careful when using them.

EXAMPLE

Words		Definitions
already	(adverb)	by this time
all ready	(adjective)	prepared
breath	(noun)	air
breathe	(verb)	to inhale and exhale air
close	(verb)	shut
	(adjective)	near; dear
clothes	(noun)	items to wear
cloths	(noun)	pieces of fabric
dairy	(noun)	shop where milk products are sold
diary	(noun)	daily record or journal
desert	(noun)	land without water
	(verb)	to leave alone
dessert	(noun)	last course of a meal; sweets
loose	(adjective)	free; not held tightly
lose	(verb)	to misplace; to fail to win
quiet	(adjective)	not noisy
quit	(verb)	to stop or leave
quite	(adverb)	completely; rather

Activity A Write the word or words in parentheses that complete each sentence correctly.

1. We've packed our things, and we're (already, all ready) for our trip.

2. The train was (already, all ready) at the station when we got there.

3. I cannot hold my (breath, breathe) for very long.

4. Open your mouth and (breath, breathe) in the fresh, country air.

5. Please (close, clothes, cloths) the window.

6. You can dust the furniture with one of the old dusting (close, clothes, cloths).

7. Don't sit too (close, clothes, cloths) to the open window.

8. Brittany writes in her (dairy, diary) every night.

9. I bought some cheese at the (dairy, diary).

10. I served the fruit for (desert, dessert).

11. I would never (desert, dessert) you in your time of need.

12. He will (loose, lose) his job if business doesn't pick up soon.

13. The clown's pants were so (loose, lose) they kept falling down.

14. There is nothing (quiet, quit, quite) as refreshing as a morning swim in the sea.

15. Ben will (quiet, quit, quite) his job if he does not get a raise.

Using What You've Learned

Correct the spelling of the underlined words in this paragraph.

  The diner is <u>quite</u> most <u>afternoones.</u> In the evening, however, people talk <u>noisyly</u>. Jean and Al often <u>meat four</u> lunch <u>hear.</u> Last <u>weak,</u> on <u>Febuary</u> 9, Al <u>stoped</u> in late. Jean was <u>worryed,</u> but she felt <u>releived</u> when her <u>freind</u> arrived. Al told Jean not to worry since he would never <u>dessert</u> her. He had gone <u>shoping</u> to buy something <u>four</u> his <u>nieghbor's</u> <u>childern.</u> Al also bought some new <u>cloose</u> to wear to work next week. Jean had <u>all ready</u> eaten and was having <u>friut</u> for <u>desert.</u> Al ordered iced tea because he cannot have <u>diary</u> products.

Adverbs can compare when, where, and how things happen. Add *-er* to an adverb to compare one thing to one other thing. Add *-est* to an adverb to compare two or more things.

EXAMPLE

Adverb	Comparing with One	Comparing with Two or More
quick	quicker	quickest
slow	slower	slowest

Some adverbs change their form to make comparisons. The adverb *well* means "in the right way." Don't confuse the adverb *well* with the adjective *good*.

Communication Connection

Many people are scared to speak in front of a group. Here are three ways to feel more comfortable speaking in front of others:

- On a sheet of paper, write what you are going to say.

- Practice your speech in front of a mirror until you know all of the words. Then, practice in front of one or two people.

- Relax before you give your speech

EXAMPLE

Adverb	Comparing with One	Comparing with Two or More
well	better	best

Activity A On your paper, write the correct form of the adverb in parentheses to complete each sentence.

1. Andy spoke (good, well) in the first round of the speech competition.

2. He did a little (better, best) in the next round.

3. He spoke the (better, best) in the final round.

4. Amy did (good, well) in math on Monday.

5. Her friend did (better, best) than she did on Tuesday.

More

Most

Less

Least

Use *more* and *most* and *less* and *least* to make comparisons with adverbs that end in *-ly*.

EXAMPLE

Adverb	Comparing with One	Comparing with Two or More
easily	more easily	most easily
	less easily	least easily
suddenly	more suddenly	most suddenly
	less suddenly	least suddenly
neatly	more neatly	most neatly
	less neatly	least neatly

Activity B Write the correct form of the adverb in parentheses to complete each sentence.

1. Mario's new car runs (more, most) smoothly than his old car.

2. It reached 65 miles per hour (more, most) quickly than his old car.

3. It burns oil (less, least) rapidly than his old car, too.

4. Mario's friends like his old car, but they like his new car (better, best).

5. Beth finishes her homework (faster, fastest) than I do.

6. Of all the teams in the league, our team worked (harder, hardest).

7. Joanna works (more, most) happily at her job than Ellie does.

8. Paul moves swiftly; Josh moves (more, most) swiftly.

9. When the four team members ran around the track, Brenda ran the distance (more, most) easily.

10. Jack handles eggs (more, most) carefully than he handles bread.

Chapter 12 R E V I E W

Part A Use the words from the Word Bank to complete sentences 1–3.

1. A word that means "one" is _____.
2. A word that means "more than one" is _____.
3. A _____ is a word that sounds like another word but has a different meaning and spelling.

Part B Change the nouns in bold to plural nouns. Write the plural nouns on your paper.

4. Behind the barn, two **calf** chewed on some **bush**.
5. Inside the barn, **mouse** sank their **tooth** into stray **kernel** of corn.
6. **Fly** buzz.
7. Some **child** ride **bus** to their **school**.
8. **Day** go by, and the **leaf** turn red and yellow.
9. During the summer, the lake is full of **goose**.
10. The chef bought three new **knife** at the cooking store.
11. The **monkey** climbed to the top of the **tree**.
12. Ty checked both **library** and made **copy** of his **note**.
13. Beyond those **hill** lie two large **valley**.

Part C Write the word in parentheses that has the correct spelling.

14. Craig and Lucy had an (arguement, argument).
15. Anton's two sisters (skiped, skipped) rope in the park.
16. Sharon thought the computer game was (awful, aweful).
17. "What a (lovly, lovely) idea," said Ruth.
18. At the party, Zoe saw three (famous, fameous) people.
19. (Either, Iether) we go to the movies now or we go later.
20. As a boy, Mr. Cho was always into (mischeif, mischief).
21. The walls are white, and the (cieling, ceiling) is blue.
22. The (doctor, docter) took blood from Allen's (vien, vein).
23. Tammy will (receive, recieve) news from her (friend, freind).

Part D Rewrite the paragraph. Choose the word in parentheses that has the correct spelling and that completes the sentence correctly.

Adam and Caroline traveled west **24.** (threw, through) the hot **25.** (desert, dessert). **26.** (Sum, Some) **27.** (families, familys) in the wagon train were **28.** (weak, week) from hunger and thirst. Adam **29.** (new, knew) few wild animals were **30.** (hear, here).

The **31.** (skies, skys) were clear. **32.** (Their, There) was no **33.** (break, brake) in the heat during the **34.** (dais, days). Later, at the water **35.** (whole, hole), **36.** (their, there) was **37.** (piece, peace) and **38.** (quite, quiet) among the **39.** (hoarses, horses).

At night, the travelers **40.** (heard, herd) **41.** (wolfs, wolves) beyond the light of the campfires. The sleep of these **42.** (mans, men) and women was **43.** (breif, brief), and they were **44.** (carful, careful) about their **45.** (safety, safty). At least, they **46.** (received, recieved) cool night air for **47.** (relief, releif).

Part E Choose the letter of the word or phrase that correctly completes each sentence.

48. My sister smiled _____ than I did.

   A cheerfullier   **C** most cheerfully

   B cheerfulliest   **D** more cheerfully

49. This is the _____ movie I have ever seen.

   A best   **B** better   **C** good   **D** well

50. The students sang _____ than they did yesterday.

   A more louder   **C** louder

   B less louder   **D** loudest

Test-Taking Tip If you have to choose the correct word to complete a sentence, read the sentence using each of the choices given. Then choose the word that fits the sentence best.

13 Fine-Tuning Your Writing

Look around you. Is there something you would like to change or improve? Is your car in good shape? It might run better if it had a tune-up. New spark plugs will fire at the right time to help the car get better mileage and prevent engine damage. Clean battery terminals might help the car start more easily. Changing the oil will protect the engine. A wax and polish could make the car shine.

You can fine-tune your writing so that it works better and flows more smoothly. Changing words and adding details can make your sentences more interesting. Rearranging sentences in a paragraph can make your ideas easier to follow and understand. Correcting mistakes in punctuation, spelling, and grammar will add polish to your writing and make it shine.

In this chapter, you will practice ways to improve your writing.

Goals for Learning

♦ To make subjects agree with verbs and pronouns agree with nouns

♦ To identify improperly written sentences

♦ To rewrite sentences to improve them

♦ To avoid the use of nonstandard English

♦ To use standard English to speak and to write

Agreement

The rule that a singular subject has a singular verb and a plural subject has a plural verb

You have learned that every sentence has a subject and a verb. The rule of **agreement** states that a verb must agree in number with its subject. A singular subject takes a singular verb. A plural subject takes a plural verb.

EXAMPLE

Singular	He eats.
Plural	They eat.
Singular	Aziza plays the guitar.
Plural	The two friends play the guitar.
Singular	The tiger runs fast.
Plural	Tigers run fast.

Do not be confused by plural nouns in titles. The title of a book, poem, song, movie, or play is singular.

EXAMPLE

Purple Bunnies is a silly TV show.
(Although *bunnies* is a plural noun, the subject *Purple Bunnies* names one TV show. The singular subject takes the singular verb *is*.)

Do not be confused by plural nouns in phrases, clauses, or appositives that come between the subject and verb.

EXAMPLE

The neighbor of my two cousins teaches history at our school.
(*Neighbor* is the singular subject. It takes the singular verb *teaches*.)

A jar that contains nails falls off the shelf.
(*Jar* is the singular subject. It takes the singular verb *falls*.)

The girl, one of three performers, smiles proudly for the audience.
(*Girl* is the singular subject. It takes the singular verb *smiles*.)

**Classifier
(He, Him)**

Eats

He eats.

Activity A Copy the sentences on your paper. Underline the subject, and circle the verb. Then write whether the subject and verb are *singular* or *plural*.

1. A small child plays with the toy.

2. Many children ride on the bus.

3. His store, which sells chairs, opens for business today.

4. Alice, a swim teacher for young children, works for the town.

5. Sheep from Ted's ranch graze on the grassy hill.

Activity B On your paper, write the verb in parentheses that agrees with the subject.

1. A woman with twin boys (buy, buys) a dozen eggs.

2. The eggs (come, comes) from a local farm.

3. Many hens (lays, lay) eggs.

4. A farmer (collects, collect) the eggs.

5. Farmers (sells, sell) the eggs to grocery stores.

Activity C Rewrite and edit this paragraph. Correct the agreement of subjects and verbs. Improve the sentences by combining them or changing their order.

> The roads across America is busy. Vehicles of all kinds drives on the highways. A trip to distant places are fun for families. People likes all the parks and beach and mountain in our country Some national parks has a few wolf and bear. When people respects wildlife, all living things is safe. Then people enjoys the outdoor life.

There are some things to keep in mind to avoid making common mistakes with subject-verb agreement.

A compound subject connected by *and* always takes a plural verb. Pay careful attention when the first part of a compound subject is plural and the second part is singular.

> **EXAMPLE**   The singers and the musicians are performing.
> The students and their teacher listen carefully.

In a sentence that begins with the adverb *here* or *there,* the subject follows the verb. Find the subject. If the subject is singular, it takes a singular verb. If the subject is plural, it takes a plural verb.

> **EXAMPLE**   Singular   There goes a very long train.
> Plural   There go two very long trains.
> Plural   There go a train and a bus.

In a question, the subject often follows the verb or comes between the helping verb and main verb. Find the subject. If the subject is singular, it takes a singular verb. If the subject is plural, it takes a plural verb.

> **EXAMPLE**   Singular   Is your brother coming with us?
> Plural   Where are the girl and her cat?
> Plural   Do the students know the words of the poem?

Writing Tip

To check subject-verb agreement in sentences starting with *here* or *there* or in questions, try this. Switch the word order so the subject comes first.

Example
A very long train goes there.

Your brother is coming with us?

Activity A Write each sentence. Underline the subject. Choose the verb in parentheses that agrees with the subject.

1. Louis and Tim (is, are) in the choir.
2. (Do, Does) the members of the choir sing this Saturday?
3. Louis and Tim (have, has) been singing in the choir for five years.
4. Here (come, comes) Mr. Whithall, the band leader.
5. When (is, are) the choir and band practicing?

Activity B On your paper, write the verb in parentheses that agrees with the subject.

1. Here (come, comes) the tow truck.
2. (Is, Are) there many cars and trucks on the highways?
3. There (has, have) been several accidents this winter.
4. There (was, were) some people stranded by the storm.
5. (Is, Are) there more snow in the weather forecast?
6. There (stand, stands) the tallest statue in the city.
7. Here (is, are) your test scores.
8. There (is, are) several large motels in the next town.
9. There (is, are) one motel with a good restaurant.
10. (Do, Does) your family and friends eat there?

Activity C Rewrite and edit this paragraph. Correct the agreement of subjects and verbs. Improve the sentences by combining them or changing their order.

Here is my friends. Here is the place where we has parties. There are the table for snacks. Here come more friends. There is a big crowd now. Are there enough food? Is there too many people? Are there room for everyone? Well, we always has good times together.

Some pronouns that refer to people and things in general are always singular. Some are always plural. Remember that a singular subject takes a singular verb. A plural subject takes a plural verb.

Singular		Plural
anybody	everything	both
anyone	neither	few
each	no one	many
either	nobody	others
everybody	somebody	several
everyone	someone	

EXAMPLE   **Singular**   Does anybody want lunch?
Plural   Many want lunch.

Some pronouns that refer to people and things in general can be either singular or plural.

all	any	most	none	some

If the noun that the pronoun refers to is singular, the pronoun is singular. If the noun is plural, the pronoun is plural.

EXAMPLE   **Singular**   Most of the lunch has been eaten.
Plural   Most of the lunches have been eaten.

The singular pronouns *everybody, everyone,* and *everything* cause special problems with subject-verb agreement. Try to think of each of these words as a group. A noun that names a group usually takes a singular verb.

EXAMPLE   Everyone is hungry.
Everybody wants lunch.
Everything in the lunches was fresh.

Activity A Write each sentence. Underline the subject. Choose the verb in parentheses that agrees with the subject.

1. Several (stand, stands) in line.

2. Few (leave, leaves) the line.

3. No one (is, are) pushing and shoving.

4. Many (wait, waits) for hours.

5. Each of the women (get, gets) concert tickets.

6. Others in line (is, are) not so lucky.

7. Everyone (want, wants) tickets for the show.

8. Neither of the lines (is, are) shorter than the other.

9. (Does, do) anyone look unhappy?

10. Everybody from our group (has, have) a ticket now.

Activity B Write each sentence. Underline the subject. Choose the verb in parentheses that agrees with the subject.

1. Several of the choir members (was, were) practicing.

2. (Have, Has) any of the members gone home yet?

3. None of that song (sound, sounds) good.

4. All of the singers (was, were) tired.

5. Each of the farmer's fields (need, needs) extra work.

6. Most of the work (has, have) been finished.

7. Some of the dogs (is, are) barking.

8. Nobody in the barns (know, knows) about the cattle contest.

9. (Do, Does) anybody know the words to this song?

10. There (is, are) some of the pizza left for you.

Many people enjoy singing in a choir.

An owner pronoun and the noun it refers to should agree in number and gender.

> **EXAMPLE** Carmelita hooked her cable to the rock.
> (The pronoun *her* refers to the singular feminine noun *Carmelita.*)
>
> Stefano and Jamilla hooked their cables to the rock.
> (The pronoun *their* refers to the compound subject *Stefano* and *Jamilla.* A compound subject is plural, so the pronoun is plural.)
>
> Each of the men took his dog to Dr. Velasquez.
> (The pronoun *his* refers to the singular pronoun *each.* The masculine form appears because *each* refers to *men,* a masculine noun that is the object of the preposition *of.*)

If you are not sure whether you should use *her* or *his,* try these choices.

- Use both *his* and *her.*
- Reword the sentence.
- Do not use a pronoun at all.

> **EXAMPLE** Each student liked his or her book.
> The students liked their books.
> Each student liked a book.

Activity A On your paper, write each sentence with an owner pronoun. Underline the word to which the pronoun refers.

1. Brenda sprained _____ ankle.

2. I gave Brenda _____ help.

3. Together, we made _____ way down the cliff.

4. Josh called home on _____ cellular phone.

5. Kevin, Josh, and Brenda remember _____ day on the mountain.

Book

Their

Student

Like

Finish

A compound subject connected by *and* is plural. It takes a plural verb. A compound subject connected by *or* can be singular or plural.

> **EXAMPLE** **Plural** Julio and Keiko work.
> **Singular** Julio or Keiko works.
> **Plural** Her cousins or her aunts work.

You can connect a compound subject with the conjunctions *either-or* or *neither-nor*.

If both parts of a compound subject are singular, use a singular verb.

> **EXAMPLE** Either Benjiro or Paulita is singing tonight.
> Neither Benjiro nor Paulita is singing tonight.

If both parts of a compound subject are plural, use a plural verb.

> **EXAMPLE** Either the sisters or their parents are singing.
> Neither the sisters nor their parents are singing.

If one part of a compound subject is singular and the other part is plural, the verb usually agrees with the part closest to the verb.

> **EXAMPLE** Either the sisters or Paulita is singing.
> Neither Paulita nor the sisters are singing.
> Paulita or the sisters are singing.

Activity B Write the verb in parentheses that agrees with the subject.

1. Neither wolves nor tigers (live, lives) in that country.
2. Neither science nor math (is, are) my favorite subject.
3. Either tools or a flashlight (fit, fits) into the space.
4. Neither the women nor Chuck (know, knows) the way.
5. Neither Ron nor his friends (was, were) hungry.

The students liked their books.

There is an easy way to check whether you have used *don't* or *doesn't* correctly. Replace with *do not* or *does not* in the sentence.

Doesn't is a contraction for *does not*. *Does* and *doesn't* go with singular subjects except *I* and *you*.

Don't is a contraction for *do not*. *Do* and *don't* go with plural subjects.

EXAMPLE

Singular	**Plural**
Maria doesn't swim.	Maria and Rosita don't swim.
The dog does swim.	The dogs do swim.
I don't swim.	We don't swim.
Don't you swim?	You two don't swim.

Activity A Complete each sentence with *don't* or *doesn't*. Write the sentences on your paper.

 1. You _____ need money at the picnic.

 2. She _____ look very happy.

 3. They _____ want any dinner.

 4. It _____ look good to me.

 5. He _____ say very much.

 6. We _____ play video games at the mall.

 7. A hot summer _____ seem short.

 8. Sandy and Ed _____ own a fax machine.

 9. A pleasant vacation _____ seem long.

10. It _____ matter.

11. Grass and flowers _____ grow well in this dry climate.

12. A big truck _____ stop fast.

13. They _____ live in this town.

14. He _____ go to this school.

15. _____ she want breakfast?

Using *this, that, these,* and *those* can make your sentences more interesting.

Remember not to use the contractions *doesn't* and *don't* in reports and other formal writing.

Use *doesn't* with *this* and *that*.

EXAMPLE   That window doesn't open easily.
This plant doesn't have flowers.

Use *don't* with *these* and *those*.

EXAMPLE   These tables don't match each other.
Those pictures don't hang straight.

Activity B Complete each sentence with *don't* or *doesn't*. Write the sentences on your paper.

1. This book _____ belong to me.

2. That one _____ belong to me, either.

3. These_____ look good.

4. Those _____ look very good, either.

5. This _____ look much better.

6. _____ that seem like a good idea?

7. This room _____ look good.

8. That lamp _____ work.

9. These drapes _____ go with the sofa.

10. That carpet _____ go with anything.

Activity C Rewrite and edit this paragraph. Correct the agreement of subjects and verbs. Improve the sentences by combining them or changing their order.

My computer don't work good. Either the program or the machine aren't working right. When I call a repair service, they doesn't know nothing. My computer teacher at school help me. Now my computer do work. My printer are jammed. Neither my teacher nor my friends knows about that problem.

Writing Tip

Always proofread your writing carefully to make sure you have really said what you mean. Are words and phrases near the words and phrases they describe? Would the placement of any words or phrases confuse your reader?

The meaning of an entire sentence can change when you move a word or a phrase. Read over your sentences. Be sure the sentence means what you want it to mean.

EXAMPLE   Consuela just met Abdul at the library.
(Here *just* tells when Consuela met Abdul at the library. They met *just* now.)

Consuela met just Abdul at the library.
(Here *just* tells whom Consuela met at the library. She met *just* Abdul and no one else.)

Only Emiko knows the third answer.
(Here *only* means no one but Emiko knows the third answer.)

Emiko knows only the third answer.
(Here *only* means Emiko knows the third answer, but she does not know any other answers.)

Emiko knows the only answer.
(Here *only* means there is one answer, and Emiko knows it.)

Activity A On your paper, explain the difference in meaning between the sentences in each group.

1. Only Jenny looked out the window.
Jenny looked only out the window.
Jenny looked out the only window.

2. Sarah just suggested that Janine have a sandwich.
Sarah suggested that Janine have just a sandwich.

3. I just brought in the CD player.
I brought in just the CD player.

4. Dee earned just twenty dollars.
Just Dee earned twenty dollars.
Dee just earned twenty dollars.

5. That bank stays open late only on Thursdays.
Only that bank is open late on Thursdays.

Try to place phrases close to the words they describe. A sentence may not make sense or its meaning may be unclear if you misplace a phrase.

Unclear	The reporters talked about cooking at work. (Did the reporters want to cook at work? Probably they did not.)
Clear	The reporters talked at work about cooking.
Unclear	The boy saw an elephant on the way home. (Was the elephant on its way home? It's not likely.)
Clear	On the way home, the boy saw a elephant.

Activity B Find the misplaced phrase in each sentence. Rewrite the sentence so that its meaning is clear.

1. Mom drove Alice to the party in her car.

2. A present was brought by Alice in brown paper.

3. The children told stories about ghosts in the room.

4. Alice wandered into the room acting shy and nervous.

5. Casey asked Alice to sit next to her smiling.

6. The animals looked at me in the zoo through the bars.

7. The rabbit hid under the bush with the little white tail.

8. The elephant sprayed the man on the bench with a trunkful of water.

9. Some people waited beside the lion cage with strollers.

10. The monkeys watched Kate swinging on the tree branches.

Communication Connection

People use body language to show how they feel. A shy, nervous person might hold his or her head down. Smiling is a sign that a person is happy and friendly.

You can see a variety of animals at the zoo.

You probably speak differently to your teachers and your boss than you do to your friends. Most people tend to use a more relaxed form of the English language when speaking to family and friends. In some cases, however, this relaxed attitude results in dialogue that has little or no meaning for listeners.

> **EXAMPLE**
>
> "Well, I'd like this job and, well, I think you should hire me and, well, I hope you will."
>
> "So, like, if you hire me and, like, I'm sick, like, do I get, like, sick leave?"
>
> "You know, I think we need longer, you know, breaks, you know, because, you know, we're on our feet, you know, all day."

The repetition of *well*, *like*, and *you know* in the examples gets in the way of the speaker's message. Notice how the removal of these words makes the speaker's meaning clear.

> **EXAMPLE**
>
> "I'd like this job, and I think you should hire me. I hope you will."
>
> "If you hire me, and I get sick, do I get sick leave?"
>
> "I think we need longer breaks because we're on our feet all day."

People sometimes divide the English language into two types.

- Standard English is the English you read in most textbooks and hear on TV and radio news programs. Standard English follows the rules of English grammar. It is always acceptable and correct.

- Nonstandard English is the English you may use with your friends. You may also hear characters in TV shows and movies speaking it. Writers may use it in dialogue to make their characters sound like real people. Nonstandard English follows current styles of speech. It often contains slang and regional expressions. It does not always follow the rules of grammar. For these reasons, it is not acceptable to use nonstandard English in formal situations.

> You might also find nonstandard English in friendly letters or e-mail. You should never use nonstandard English in reports, presentations, or business letters.

Here are examples of standard and nonstandard English.

EXAMPLE	Standard English	Nonstandard English
	She isn't here.	She ain't here.
	Where were you?	Where were you at?
	Jorge did well.	Jorge done good.
	He might have done it.	He might of done it.
	She will try to go.	She will try and go.
	He's been everywhere.	He's been everywheres.
	Serafina went all the way down the street.	Serafina went a ways down the street.

Activity A Read what Pam tells her friend Beth about Ben, who works with her. Rewrite Pam's dialogue on your paper. Use standard English.

I saw Ben in Shipping. So I go, "Hi," and he goes, "Hi yourself." Then he goes, "How you doing?" and I go, "Not bad. How about you?" So he goes, "Okay, sorta. I'm sorta hanging loose between things."

Activity B On your paper, rewrite the following dialogue. Use standard English.

Colleen has done collected dolls from all over the world. She says, "I ain't never gonna stop. Like, I like dolls from everywheres on earth."

Then I says, "Where did you find this one at?"

Then she says, "Like, you know, in a store in New York. It's from like Tibet."

Then I says, "I should of started a doll collection, too."

Then she says, "I ain't too busy to try and help you."

Then I says, "Thanks. You done real good with your set."

Good writers may edit and rewrite a story or an article several times before they are satisfied. The edit and rewrite stages of the writing process are important, and you should never rush or skip them.

> You may not be sure what to edit or rewrite. Ask a classmate, teacher, friend, or family member to read your story or article. Readers often have valuable suggestions about what to change or correct.

Activity A Read the first draft of a letter by an unhappy worker to her boss. On your paper, rewrite the paragraph to improve it. Use standard English. Correct mistakes in grammar, spelling, and punctuation.

> I got several problems with my job I ain't had enough time to do it right. I got too much to do. I beleive I need more time to complete this job well. Maybe two more weeks. I can do it, but I needs more time. I no the company wants good work and like I wants more time so's its done good.

Activity B Write the verb in parentheses that agrees with the subject.

1. "Smiles" (is, are) a nice song.

2. Smiles (is, are) nice.

3. "Rainy Days" (is, are) a sad piece of music.

4. *Happy Guys* (was, were) a funny movie.

5. The happy guys (was, were) played by good actors.

Activity C Match the terms with their descriptions. Write the number and its correct letter on your paper.

Terms	Descriptions
1. several	**A** follows current styles of speech
2. everybody	**B** names an entire group
3. agree	**C** names more than one
4. standard English	**D** follows rules of grammar in writing and speaking
5. nonstandard English	**E** what subjects and verbs need to do

Try to avoid using sentences that ask *where* someone or something is by using the word *at.*

Activity D Rewrite these sentences on your paper. Use standard English.

1. I know where it's at.

2. Where you at?

3. Let me know where you're at tonight.

4. Tell me where Joe's going to be at tomorrow.

5. Look where I'm at now!

6. Where are you at with your homework?

7. If you want good music, that radio station is where it's at.

8. Where have Ben and Todd been at lately?

9. Where have you been at while I was gone?

10. How can I know where you're at if you don't call?

Activity E Edit and rewrite these sentences. Use standard English.

1. I ain't never been nowhere in my life.

2. I'm like, "Where you at?"

3. He don't go there no more.

4. So I go, "No way! I ain't doing that!"

5. We doesn't set on the porch no more.

Using What You've Learned

Write a paragraph about a conversation that you had with a friend. Edit and rewrite your work, checking for nonstandard English and incorrect grammar, spelling, and punctuation.

Chapter 13 R E V I E W

Part A Write the verb in parentheses that agrees with the subject.

1. Bill and Jenny (is, are) two old friends.
2. They (have, has) flown jets for several years.
3. Both (are, is) checked out for carrier landings.
4. Bill and Jenny (do, does) most of their flying together.
5. Their teamwork (have, has) earned them a fine military record.

Part B Copy each sentence. Underline each subject. Choose the correct form of the verb. Do not be confused by nouns in prepositional phrases.

6. Someone (has, have) answered all the questions.
7. Others (has, have) not finished the test.
8. Most (study, studies) hard for that class.
9. Many (earn, earns) good grades.
10. Each member of our class (take, takes) three tests today.
11. All of the tests (is, are) an hour long.
12. One of the tests (cover, covers) science.
13. Rod and his friends (learn, learns) what the teacher expects from the class.
14. Each of the cooks (is, are) trained well.
15. No one (complain, complains) about this food.

Part C On your paper, explain the difference in meaning between the sentences.

16. Graciana gave just Kareem a present on his birthday.
    Graciana just gave Kareem a present on his birthday.
    Graciana gave Kareem just a present on his birthday.

Part D Rewrite these sentences correctly on your paper.

17. jill says that its fun surfing the internet but she don't know where shes at

18. antonio says your right but i ain't got no modem

19. by one of them modems at the big store next to the park with the red neon sign said jill

20. their like easy to use said jill.

21. she said that alls you have to do is like plug it in

22. the computer recieves all them signals jill told antonio

23. antonio said i no where the store's at and I'm gonna go

Part E Write the pronoun in parentheses that agrees with the subject.

24. One of the men has (his, their) own service station.

25. Each of the women gave (her, their) thanks for the good job the men did.

26. Most of the people give (his, their) support to local shops.

Part F Write the letter of the word or phrase that correctly completes each sentence.

27. The rule of _____ says that a singular subject has a singular verb and a plural subject has a plural verb.

    A verbs   **B** number   **C** action   **D** agreement

28. That movie _____ terrible.

    A were   **B** are   **C** is   **D** am

29. Neither this store nor that one _____ DVDs.

    A sell   **B** sells   **C** are selling   **D** have sold

30. Either the twins or their sister _____ a TV.

    A owns   **B** own   **C** have owned   **D** do own

Test-Taking Tip When studying for a test, use a highlighter to mark things you want to remember. To review your notes quickly, look at the highlighted words.

The word *process* makes writing sound as if it is a simple set of steps every writer follows. In fact, every writer follows his or her own set of steps. But every writer must answer the same questions: *What do I write about? How do I organize my ideas? What do I leave in? What do I take out? How can I make my writing better?* Answering these questions is part of every writer's writing process. The process discussed below gives you guidelines to follow when you write.

Prewriting

Choosing a Topic

Some writers think this is the hardest part of writing. Certainly it is a very important part. Without a good topic, you have nowhere to go with your writing. Here are some ways to look for a topic:

- Think about people you know, places you have seen, and activities you enjoy.
- Think about memories or experiences from your past.
- Read newspapers and magazines. Listen to the radio. Watch TV.
- Write down anything that comes to mind. You may find an idea as you freewrite. When you freewrite, you write topics as you think of them. This is also called *brainstorming*.
- Talk to other people about your ideas. They may offer suggestions.
- Ask questions about a subject. A question can be a good topic to investigate.

- Choose a topic that you feel strongly about. It may be something you like. It may be something you dislike.
- Use a graphic organizer such as a map, diagram, chart, or web. The details in a graphic organizer may provide a good topic. Here is an example of a graphic organizer you can use as you prewrite.

Four-Column Chart

Main Topic

Subtopic	Subtopic	Subtopic	Subtopic
details about the main topic	details about the main topic	details about the main topic	details about the main topic

You can use a four-column chart to organize your thoughts before you begin writing. It will help you see the relationship among ideas. Write your main topic as the title of the chart. Then write a subtopic at the top of each column. Use the columns beneath each subtopic to record details that you can use to support your main topic.

Developing a Topic

Once you have chosen your topic, you need to find information about it. There are several kinds of details:

- Facts
- Reasons
- Examples
- Sensory images
- Stories or events

Where do you get these details? First, look back at anything you wrote when you were thinking about topics—notes, charts, webs, maps, and so on. To find more details, you might do the following:

- Research
- Interview
- Observe
- Remember
- Imagine

Before you begin to write your first draft, you need to answer two more questions:

- What is my reason for writing?
- Who is my audience?

Your reason for writing may be to entertain, to inform, to persuade, or a combination of these purposes. Your audience may be your classmates, your friends, or any other group of people. Knowing your reason for writing helps you focus. Knowing your audience helps you choose the information to include.

Drafting

Now it is time to write your first draft. In a first draft, you put down all your ideas on paper. Some writers make an outline or a plan first and follow it as they write. Other writers write their ideas in no particular order and then rearrange them later. Use whatever method works best for you.

Try to write the whole draft at once. Do not stop to rearrange or change anything. You can do that after you have finished the draft. Remember, a first draft will be rough.

How can you arrange your details? Here are some suggestions:

- Main idea and supporting details
- Chronological, or time, order
- Order of importance
- Comparison and contrast

How can you begin and end your writing? A good introduction should tell readers what they will be reading about. It should also catch their attention. You might begin with:

- A story
- A fact
- A question
- A quotation

A good conclusion tells readers that the writing is coming to a close. Generally, it makes a statement about what you have written. You might end with:

- A summary
- A suggestion
- The last event in a sequence

Revising

Now it is time to revise your draft. When you revise, you try to improve what you have written. You decide what you like and do not like. You decide what you want to change and how you will change it. You might add or take out words. You might rearrange sentences or paragraphs. Here are some tips for revising:

- Set your draft aside for a while. Then read it. This will help you see your writing in a new way.
- Read your draft aloud. This will help you hear awkward sentences and see places where information is missing.
- Ask someone else to read your draft. Encourage the reader to tell you what you have done well and what needs work.
- Ask yourself (and your reader) questions about your draft. For example:
    - —Is my main idea clear?
    - —Have I arranged my ideas in a way that makes sense?
    - —Is there any information that I should include?
    - —Is there any information that I should leave out?

Now, using your comments and your reader's comments, rewrite your draft. Then read your second draft and revise it. You may have to write several drafts before you have one that you like.

Proofreading

Once you have a draft you like, proofread it. When you proofread, you look for and correct mistakes in spelling, grammar, punctuation, and capitalization. These kinds of mistakes distract your reader. Remember, you want your reader to notice your ideas, not your mistakes. Here are some suggestions to help you proofread:

- Make a checklist of things to look for. For example:
    - —Did I spell words correctly?
    - —Did I write complete sentences?
    - —Did I vary my sentences?
    - —Did I use vivid verbs and specific details?
    - —Do my subjects and verbs agree?
    - —Did I use correct capitalization?
    - —Did I use correct end punctuation?

- Use a computer spell checker, but remember, it cannot catch some spelling errors.
- Ask someone else to proofread your work.
- Proofread more than once. Look for a different kind of mistake each time.
- Read your work aloud. You may hear mistakes.
- Set your writing aside. Proofread it later. You may see mistakes more clearly.
- Keep a thesaurus nearby. It will help you replace words that you have used too frequently.
- Keep a dictionary and a grammar reference book nearby. You may have questions that they can help answer.

To make your proofreading faster and easier to follow, use proofreaders' marks. Draw the mark at the place where you want to make the correction. Here are some common proofreaders' marks.

Proofreaders' Marks	
ℊ Delete or take out	⌄ Insert an apostrophe
ⓈⓅ Spell out	⌄⌄ Insert quotation marks
∧ Insert	ℓ𝒸 Change to lowercase
# Insert space	≡ Change to capital letter
⊙ Insert a period	◡ Close up; take out space
⋏ Insert a comma	¶ Begin a paragraph
⋏ Insert a semicolon	𝓉𝓇 Transpose letter or words

Publishing

Think of publishing as presenting and sharing your writing with others. Many writers get their writing published in a newspaper or magazine or as a book. However, there are other ways to publish your writing:

- Get together with other writers. Take turns reading your work aloud and discussing it.
- Send your writing to a school or community newspaper or magazine.
- Give copies of your work to anyone who is interested in reading it, including family members and friends.
- Post your work on the classroom bulletin board.
- Make a classroom newspaper or magazine several times a year. Use the newspaper or magazine to present things that you and your classmates write.

Each time you write, think about the writing process you used. Ask yourself the following questions: *What would I do the same next time? What would I do differently? What parts of the process do I need to work on?* Use the answers to these questions to help you the next time you write.

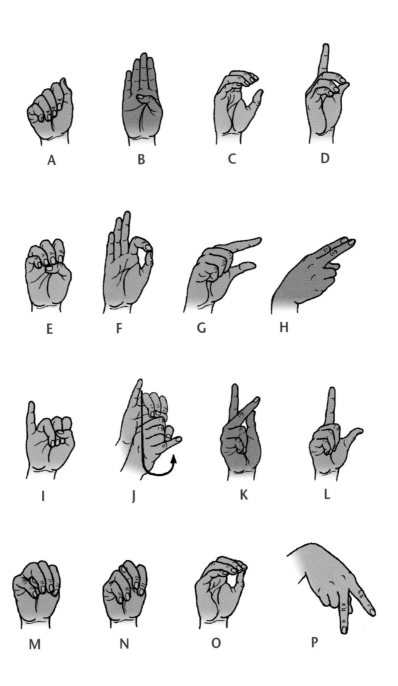

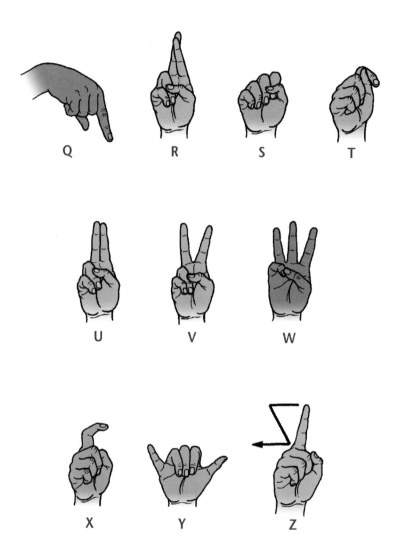

Q   R   S   T

U   V   W

X   Y   Z

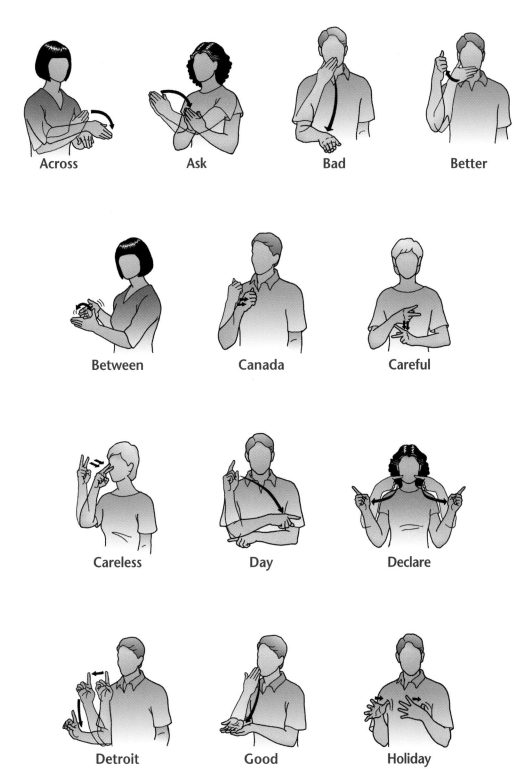

Across

Ask

Bad

Better

Between

Canada

Careful

Careless

Day

Declare

Detroit

Good

Holiday

Hopping

In

Less

Least

Lovely

More

Most

President

Spring

Summer

Telephones

Their

There

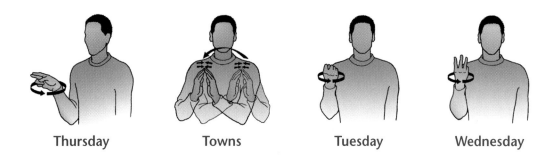

Thursday   Towns   Tuesday   Wednesday

What   Where   Who

Why   Winter   With

Worse   Yell   Your

Glossary

A

Abbreviation—(ə brē vē ā′ shən) short form of a word (p. 194)

Abstract noun—(ab′ strakt noun) a word that names something that cannot be seen or touched (p. 77)

Action verb—(ak′ shən vėrb) a word that tells what the subject of a sentence does (p. 10)

Adjective—(aj′ ik tiv) a word that describes a noun (p. 8)

Adjective object complement—(aj′ ik tiv ob′ jikt kom′ plə mənt) an adjective that describes the direct object (p. 118)

Adjective prepositional phrase—(aj′ ik tiv prep ə zish′ ə nəl frāz) a prepositional phrase that describes a noun (p. 30)

Adjective subject complement—(aj′ ik tiv sub′ jikt kom′ plə mənt) one or more adjectives in the predicate that describe the subject (p. 136)

Adverb—(ad′ vėrb) a word that describes a verb, an adjective, or another adverb (p. 12)

Adverb prepositional phrase—(ad′ vėrb prep ə zish′ ə nəl frāz) a prepositional phrase that describes a verb (p. 34)

Agreement—(ə grē′ mənt) the rule that a singular subject has a singular verb and a plural subject has a plural verb (p. 262)

Apostrophe—(ə pos′ trə fē) a punctuation mark in an owner's name (p. 94)

Appositive—(ə poz′ ə tiv) a word or group of words that follows a noun and explains the noun or gives another name to the noun (p. 122)

Article—(är′ tə kəl) a word that points out a noun (p. 9)

B

Body—(bod′ ē) the message part of a letter (p. 234)

C

Capital letter—(kap′ ə təl let′ ər) a letter that is uppercase. *A* is a capital or uppercase letter; *a* is a lowercase letter (p. 4)

Capitalize—(kap′ ə tə līz) to use capital letters (p. 86)

Closing—(klō′ zing) word or phrase used before the signature in a letter (p. 234)

Colon—(kō′ lən) a punctuation mark used in time (p. 194)

Comma—(kom′ ə) a punctuation mark used to set apart one or more words (p. 22)

Common noun—(kom′ ən noun) the name of a general type of person, place, or thing (p. 44)

Comparative—(kəm par′ ə tiv) an adjective that compares two nouns (p. 152)

Complete predicate—(kəm plēt′ pred′ ə kit) the whole part of a sentence that tells what the subject is doing (p. 18)

Complete subject—(kəm plēt′ sub′ jikt) the whole part of a sentence that tells who or what the sentence is about (p. 18)

Complex sentence—(kom′ pleks sen′ təns) a sentence that includes both an independent clause and a dependent clause (p. 206)

Compound—(kom′ pound) two or more words, phrases, or ideas joined by a conjunction (p. 60)

Compound-complex sentence—(kom′ pound kom′ pleks sen′ təns) a sentence with two or more independent clauses and one or more dependent clauses (p. 207)

Compound direct object—(kom′ pound də rekt′ ob′ jikt) two or more direct objects joined by a conjunction (p. 70)

Compound object of preposition—(kom′ pound ob′ jikt ov prep ə zish′ ən) two or more objects of one preposition joined by a conjunction (p. 56)

Compound predicate—(kom´ pound pred´ ə kit) two or more verbs joined by a conjunction (p. 54)

Compound sentence—(kom´ pound sen´ təns) a sentence made up of two or more complete sentences joined by a conjunction (p. 58)

Compound subject—(kom´ pound sub´ jikt) two or more subjects joined by a conjunction (p. 52)

Compound subject complement—(kom´ pound sub´ jikt kom´ plə mənt) two or more subject complements joined by a conjunction (p. 142)

Concrete noun—(kon´ krēt noun) a word that names something that can be seen or touched (p. 77)

Conjunction—(kən jungk´ shən) a word that joins two or more words, phrases, or ideas in a sentence (p. 50)

Contraction—(kən trak´ shən) a word formed when two words are put together and letters are left out (p. 174)

D

Dependent clause—(di pen´ dənt klòz) a group of words that does not form a complete thought and cannot stand alone (p. 206)

Descriptive paragraph—(di skrip´ tiv par´ ə graf) a paragraph that describes a person, place, or thing (p. 224)

Dialogue—(dī´ ə lòg) conversation between two or more characters in a story (p. 231)

Direct object—(də rekt´ ob´ jikt) a noun or pronoun that receives action directly from the verb (p. 68)

Direct quotation—(də rekt´ kwō tā´ shən) the exact words that someone says (p. 210)

Double negative—(dub´ əl neg´ ə tiv) the mistake of using two words that mean "no" in one sentence (p. 190)

E

Edit—(ed´ it) checking written work for mistakes (p. 106)

Exclamation point—(ek´ sklə mā´ shən point) a punctuation mark showing strong feeling (p. 4)

F

Fragment—(frag´ mənt) a group of words that is not a complete sentence (p. 20)

Future tense—(fyü´ chər tens) the verb tense that tells about action in the future (p. 166)

G

Greeting—(grē´ ting) word or phrase used before the name or title of the person to whom a letter is sent (p. 234)

H

Heading—(hed´ ing) the address of the person writing the letter (p. 234)

Helping verb—(hel´ ping vėrb) a verb that comes before the main verb. Together, the two verbs form a verb phrase (p. 160)

Homonym—(hom´ ə nim) a word that sounds like another word but has a different meaning and spelling (p. 244)

I

Independent clause—(in di pen´ dənt klòz) a complete sentence (p. 206)

Indirect object—(in də rekt´ ob´ jikt) a noun or pronoun that takes action from the verb indirectly (p. 114)

Indirect quotation—(in də rekt´ kwō tā´ shən) what someone says but not his or her exact words (p. 210)

Interjection—(in tər jek´ shən) a word that shows feelings (p. 104)

Invitation—(in və tā´ shən) a written request (p. 221)

Pronunciation Key								
a	hat	e	let	ī	ice	ô	order	ù	put	sh	she		a in about
ā	age	ē	equal	o	hot	oi	oil	ü	rule	th	thin	ə	e in taken
ä	far	ėr	term	ō	open	ou	out	ch	child	ŦH	then		i in pencil
â	care	i	it	ò	saw	u	cup	ng	long	zh	measure		o in lemon
													u in circus

Irregular verb—(i reg´ yə lər vėrb) a verb that changes its form to form past tenses (p. 170)

L

Lead paragraph—(lēd par´ ə graf) a paragraph that introduces a news article; it tells who, what, when, where, why, and sometimes, how (p. 222)

Linking verb—(lingk´ ing vėrb) a verb that connects the subject to a word in the predicate (p. 132)

M

Memo—(mem´ ō) a clear, organized record of important facts and details (p. 220)

N

Narrative—(nar´ ə tiv) a series of paragraphs that go together to tell a story (p. 230)

Negative—(neg´ ə tiv) a word that means "no" or "not" and that stops the action of the verb (p. 168)

Nominative pronoun—(nom´ ə nə tiv prō´ noun) a pronoun used as the subject of a sentence (p. 78)

Noun—(noun) a word that names a person, place, or thing (p. 6)

Noun object complement—(noun ob´ jikt kom´ plə mənt) a noun that renames the direct object (p. 118)

Noun subject complement—(noun sub´ jikt kom´ plə mənt) a noun or pronoun in the predicate that renames the subject, as well as any words that describe the noun or pronoun (p. 132)

O

Object complement—(ob´ jikt kom´ plə mənt) a word or words that follow the direct object and describe or rename it (p. 118)

Object of the preposition—(ob´ jikt ov ŦHə prep ə zish´ ən) the noun or pronoun that follows the preposition in a prepositional phrase (p. 28)

Objective pronoun—(əb jek´ tiv prō´ noun) a pronoun that is the direct object or object of the preposition (p. 78)

Owner noun—(ō´ nər noun) a noun that owns something in a sentence (p. 94)

Owner object—(ō´ nər ob´ jekt) a noun following an owner pronoun or owner noun (p. 96)

Owner pronoun—(ō´ nər prō´ noun) a pronoun that owns something in a sentence (p. 96)

P

Paragraph—(par´ ə graf) a group of sentences about one topic (p. 224)

Past tense—(past tens) the verb tense that tells about action in the past (p. 164)

Period—(pir´ ē əd) the punctuation mark ending a sentence that makes a statement or gives a command (p. 4)

Persuasive paragraph—(pər swā´ siv par´ ə graf) a paragraph that tries to make readers believe something or do something (p. 228)

Plural—(plùr´ əl) more than one (p. 248)

Predicate—(pred´ ə kit) the part of a sentence that tells what the subject is doing (p. 4)

Preposition—(prep ə zish´ ən) a word that ties or relates a noun or pronoun to another part of the sentence (p. 28)

Prepositional phrase—(prep ə zish´ ə nəl frāz) a group of words that begins with a preposition and ends with a noun or pronoun (p. 28)

Present tense—(prez´ nt tens) the verb tense that tells about action in the present (p. 162)

Prewrite—(prē´ rīt) talking, thinking, or reading about a topic before writing (p. 106)

Process paragraph—(pros´ es par´ ə graf) a paragraph that tells how to do something (p. 226)

Pronoun—(prō´ noun) a word that takes the place of a noun (p. 78)

Proper noun—(prop´ ər noun) the name of a specific person, place, or thing (p. 44)

Punctuation—(pungk chü ā´ shən) marks in a sentence that tell readers when to pause or stop (p. 22)

Q

Question mark—(kwes´ chən märk) a punctuation mark that ends a sentence asking a question (p. 4)

Question pronoun—(kwes´ chən prō´ noun) a pronoun that asks a question (p. 204)

Quotation marks—(kwō tā´ shən märks) punctuation used around the title of a part of a large work; punctuation used to begin and end a direct quotation (pp. 63, 210)

R

Regular verb—(reg´ yə lər vėrb) a verb that adds -d or -ed to form the past tense (p. 158)

Review—(ri vyü´) a writer's opinion about a movie, TV show, book, or play (p. 232)

Rewrite—(rē´ rīt) writing again until the meaning is clear (p. 106)

S

Semicolon—(sem´ i kō lən) a punctuation mark that separates two related ideas not connected by a conjunction (p. 62)

Sentence—(sen´ təns) a group of words that forms a complete thought; a sentence begins with a capital letter and ends with a period, question mark, or exclamation point (p. 4)

Sentence pattern—(sen´ təns pat´ ərn) the basic form of a sentence (p. 5)

Signature—(sig´ nə chər) the name signed by the writer of the letter (p. 234)

Simple predicate—(sim´ pəl pred´ ə kit) one or more verbs in a sentence (p. 18)

Simple subject—(sim´ pəl sub´ jikt) one or more subject nouns or pronouns in a sentence (p. 18)

Singular—(sing´ gyə lər) one (p. 248)

State-of-being verb—(stāt ov bē´ ing vėrb) a verb that tells that the subject exists, but does not show action (p. 40)

Subject

Subject—(sub´ jikt) the part of a sentence that tells who or what the sentence is about (p. 4)

Subject complement—(sub´ jikt kom´ plə mənt) one or more words in the predicate that describe the subject (p. 132)

Superlative—(sə pėr´ lə tiv) an adjective that compares three or more nouns (p. 152)

T

Tense—(tens) present, past, or future time expressed by a verb (p. 158)

Tone of voice—(tōn ov vois) the sound of speech (p. 200)

Topic—(top´ ik) the main idea of an essay or paragraph (p. 224)

Topic sentence—(top´ ik sen´ təns) a sentence that states the main idea of a paragraph (p. 224)

U

Understood subject—(un´ dər stŏŏd´ sub´ jikt) a subject that cannot be seen in a sentence (p. 100)

Understood you—(un´ dər stŏŏd´ yōō) *you* as a subject that cannot be seen in a sentence (p. 100)

V

Verb—(vėrb) a word that shows action (p. 10)

Verb phrase—(vėrb frāz) a verb and its helpers (p. 160)

W

Write—(rīt) putting ideas on paper (p. 106)

Writing process—(rī´ ting pros´ es) the use of four steps: prewrite, write, rewrite, and edit (p. 106)

Pronunciation Key

a	hat	e	let	ī	ice	ô	order	ů	put	sh	she		
ā	age	ē	equal	o	hot	oi	oil	ü	rule	th	thin		a in about
ä	far	ėr	term	ō	open	ou	out	ch	child	ᴛʜ	then	ə	e in taken
â	care	i	it	ò	saw	u	cup	ng	long	zh	measure		i in pencil
													o in lemon
													u in circus

Index

Index

Photo Credits

Cover: background, © Comstock Images; inset, © Stockbyte; p. xvi, © Romilly Lockyer/Image Bank/Getty Images; p. 1, © Myrleen Ferguson Cate/Photo Edit Inc.; p. 2, © Michael Hendrikse/International Stock; p. 5, © Patric Ramsey/International Stock; p. 23, © Murray and Associates, Inc./ PictureQuest; p. 26, © CLEO FreelancePhoto/ Photo Researchers; p. 43, © Kathy Ferguson-Johnson/PhotoEdit; p. 45, © Bachmann/Unicorn Stock; p. 48, © David Young Wolff/PhotoEdit, Inc.; p. 54, © George D. Lepp/Photo Researchers; p. 57, © Tony Freeman/PhotoEdit; p. 66, © Eric R. Berndt/Unicorn Stock; p. 75, © J Eastcott/Y. Momatiuk/Photo Researchers; p. 83, © John Sohm/PictureQuest; p. 90, © Grantpix/Index Stock Imagery; p. 93, © SW Productions/PhotoDisc/Images; p. 103, © Jim Steinberg/Photo Researchers; p. 112, © Ronny Jaques/Photo Researchers; p. 121, © SuperStock; p. 124, © Paul Conklin/PhotoEdit; p. 130, © Jean Louis-Batt/FPG International/Getty Images; p. 137, © SuperStock; p. 149, © Spencer Grant/PhotoEdit; p. 156 left, © Prentice K. Stout; p. 156 center, © Ken Cavanagh/Photo Researchers; p. 156 right, © Chad Ehlers/International Stock; p. 169, © SuperStock; p. 171, © Paul Conklin/PhotoEdit; p. 178, © Tony Freeman/PhotoEdit, Inc.; p. 183, © Bob Daemmrich/Stock Boston/PictureQuest; p. 191, © Myrleen Ferguson Cate/ PhotoEdit, Inc.; p. 198, © Kwame Zikomo/Superstock; p. 201, © PhotoLink/Getty Images, Inc.; p. 211, © Willie L. Hill/ Stock Boston/PictureQuest; p. 218, © SW Production/Index Stock Imagery; p. 225, © Kindra Clineff/Index Stock Imagery; p. 237, © Aaron Haupt/Photo Researchers; p. 240, © Scott Wm. Hanrahan/International Stock; p. 243, © Glen Allison/Stone/Getty Images; p. 253, © Tim Davis/Stone/Getty Images; p. 260, © John Michael/International Stock; p. 267, © Tom Carter/PhotoEdit; p. 273, © Gale Zucker/ Stock Boston, Inc./PictureQuest